CARE AND DISCRETION

Care and Discretion

*Social Workers' Decisions
with Delinquents*

HENRI GILLER
ALLISON MORRIS

BURNETT BOOKS
in association with ANDRE DEUTSCH

First published 1981 by
Burnett Books Limited in association
with André Deutsch Limited
105 Great Russell Street
London WC1

ISBN 0 233 972943 (hardback)
ISBN 0 233 973737 (paperback)

Printed in Great Britain by
Ebenezer Baylis & Son Limited, The Trinity Press,
Worcester, and London

Contents

Acknowledgements

We would like to thank the Department of Health and Social Security for their financial support; the various social workers, court officers, and directors of social services of the local authorities concerned for their time and thoughts. We are also grateful to Betty Arnold and Pat Cochrane who patiently transcribed the tapes of the interviews and typed the various drafts of this research. We are grateful to Messrs. Edward Arnold for permission to reproduce extracts from *Social Work Face to Face* by Stuart Rees.

Introduction

The Children and Young Persons Act of 1969 removed from magistrates the power to decide where a child who had committed an offence should be placed within the child care system. The care order, which replaced the approved school and fit person order as a means of dealing with juvenile offenders, vested the discretion to place the child in the hands of the local authority social service departments. The intention of the proponents of the 1969 Act was to develop a system which was flexible enough to provide for the needs of the multiplicity of children; a care order could involve residence in the child's parental home, with foster parents, in a community home (a former children's home), in a community home with education on the premises (a former approved school) or in any facility which the social service department thought appropriate. Nonetheless, within a year of the implementation of the 1969 Act, magistrates were complaining that social workers were using their new powers indiscriminately. Because some children were placed at home (either through the decision of the social workers involved with the child or through the lack of suitable residential facilities) magistrates, police and justices' clerks increasingly felt that the system was falling into disrepute (*see* Berlins and Wansell, 1974). It was said that such children:

> deride the powerlessness of the courts to deal with them, commit further offences after having been placed in the care of the local authority, and are led to think they can break the law with impunity (House of Commons Expenditure Committee, 1975).

Moreover, magistrates (supported by their clerks and the police) believed that social workers, by failing to secure residential treatment for children made the subject of care orders, were exacerbating the situation (*see* Sugden, 1972; *cf* Cooper, 1973). A 'moral panic' about the nature and practice of care orders was soon well established.

The extent to which this accurately reflects the state of affairs is difficult to gauge. Early attempts to defuse this 'moral panic' and to clarify these issues came from two surveys on the use of care orders for offenders undertaken by the Social Work Service Division of the D.H.S.S. (Department of Health and Social Security, 1972, 1973). After reviewing the operation of care orders in twenty local authorities in 1971 and 1972, the Department concluded that the 1969 Act had started well. It was comparatively rare for the children subject to a care order to be returned home direct from the court. Nevertheless, the surveys did note that, in respect of Community Homes with Education, 'the placing of boys took longer to achieve and in some cases . . . could not be achieved at all' (Department of Health and Social Security, 1972). Further difficulties were said to be caused by:

> requests from the schools of a local authority to find another placing for a boy or girl already at the school, and by the schools' reluctance, in some instances, to accept a boy or girl who, having been allocated and admitted to a school some time previously, had then persistently run away (Department of Health and Social Security, 1972).

However, the Department saw such problems as no more than teething troubles and felt that too much should not be made of 'isolated breakdowns in communication which could not be expected to be altogether avoided in the early stages of a new system.'

On the other hand, it is clear that the Children and Young Persons Act of 1969 has not produced the results intended. Rather than reducing the number of children who came before juvenile courts the opposite has occurred. In the juvenile courts 31% more children were proceeded against for indictable offences in 1978 than in 1970. Moreover, the response to delinquent children has changed dramatically since 1970.

Between 1970 and 1978 the number of children given detention centre orders for indictable offences increased by 231%. Similarly the number of 15 to 17 year olds remitted by juvenile court magistrates to the Crown Court for consideration of borstal training increased by 112%. At the same time, juvenile court magistrates have increased their use of nominal penalties. For example, the use of conditional discharge for indictable offences increased by 40% since 1970. Meanwhile, supervision orders and care orders, the measures intended to deal with the majority of children under the 1969 Act, have steadily declined in use since the Act came into force (by 15% and 16% respectively). In essence, the policy of community care officially endorsed by the 1969 Act has been undermined by sentencing practice in the juvenile courts.

Recent demands by magistrates, police and justices' clerks for the return to the juvenile courts of the power to make residential care orders and, more particularly, secure care orders (*see* House of Commons Expenditure Committee, 1975) must be viewed against this sentencing pattern. In explaining the disparate sentencing trends of juvenile courts since the passing of the Act, these groups have cited social service departments generally and the mechanism of the care order in particular as providing 'no effective provision' for dealing with young offenders.

Moreover, by positing the existence of a 'hard core of sophisticated young criminals' with whom the 'social services are unable to cope,' such groups are able to propose that 'the courts must have at least oversight and at best discretion to make a residential requirement in a care order' (House of Commons Expenditure Committee, 1975). For them, the essential prerequisite for effective treatment is the placement of a child in a residential facility and the power to ensure that he remains there.

This suggestion found favour with a subcommittee of the House of Commons Expenditure Committee which recommended that, when a care order was made, magistrates and social workers should agree in court on where the child should be placed. It also recommended that:

> When a juvenile already the subject of a care order appears before a court charged with an offence the court shall have the power to make, if it thinks fit, a 'secure care order' requiring the local authority to place the juvenile in secure accommodation for a period not less than that specified in the order (House of Commons Expenditure Committee, 1975).

The Government's response to these recommendations was published in a White Paper in May, 1976 (Home Office *et al*, 1976). Regarding the proposal for a 'secure care order' the White Paper explicitly accepted and reaffirmed the different functions of juvenile court magistrates and social workers which formed the foundation of the 1969 Act:

> The juvenile court is not, and cannot be, a child welfare department, and it is of great importance that local authorities should accept and shoulder undivided responsibility for looking after difficult or dangerous young people who have become their charge by reason of the court's decision . . . By restricting local authorities' discretion it would undermine the concept of the care order and limit the local authorities' responsibility for determining or providing the proper treatment of young people placed in their care.

Nonetheless, the White Paper went on to suggest that magistrates be given the power to recommend where a child under a care order should be placed, 'including a recommendation that he or she should be placed in secure accommodation' (Home Office *et al*, 1976).

Calls for residential or secure care orders continue (Magistrates' Association *et al*, 1978) and there is an increasing belief in the existence of a 'hard core of sophisticated young criminals' from whom society is said to be at risk. What is particularly interesting in these debates is that there is little empirical information about the operation of the 1969 Act in general and of the care order in particular *and* that this does not seem to matter. This lack has not prevented the Act from being made the subject of continued criticism and suggested reform. It is *believed* that delinquent children have become more difficult and that social work efforts are not sufficient to deal with such children. We do not, however, *know* this.

It is against this background that this research emerged. Who are the children made subject to a care order? What happens to them once the care order is made? Do most children return to their own homes? How long do they remain in the care of the local authority? Are such children more 'difficult' than those within the previous system? How prevalent is re-offending, absconding and violence among such children? Without such basic information, further debates and suggestions for reform will be misinformed and may be misguided. The current project, unfortunately, can answer these questions only to a very limited extent because it was a feasibility study. In all, there were seventy-nine children in our sample. They are all children made the subject of a care order on offence grounds between 1st November, 1978 and 31st January, 1979 in the 13 social service departments of the Inner London Boroughs.* Chapter One provides a profile of these children and their career in care over a period of 6 months. This information was abstracted from the files of local authority social services departments on each child.

Such information does not, however, tell us how the decisions which are presented in official reports and statistics are made. Because such reports and statistics conceal the processes involved in the making of such decisions, not only can much information be lost, but the inferences drawn may be misplaced. Certainly research in this area has been forced to surmise on the real difficulties which lie behind the factual information which has been collected. For example, the researchers in the recent report on the work of an assessment centre ('First Year at Fairfield Lodge', Social Services Research and Intelligence Unit, Portsmouth Polytechnic, 1976) realised the limitations of their methodology of relying on official reports alone when they commented that awareness of

---

*Some of the social workers in these departments were on strike during part of the research period. All of them were interviewed on resuming work and only one disagreed with the care order being made.

shortages (in residential placements) may have influenced the original recommendations.

An examination of how social workers make decisions within the statutory framework of the care order makes the information obtained in the official reports explicable. For example, while it may be accurate that many children are sent home after being made the subject of a care order, this does not explain *why* such decisions are made. Also, the average length of time which a child spends subject to a care order may be no more than two years; but this does not explain the *reasons* which go towards deciding to discharge the order. Similarly, the social worker's perception of the 'failure' of a placement is problematic; questions of how these decisions are reached and how concepts such as 'difficult' or 'disruptive' are created and applied need to be investigated. A statistical analysis of case files may show that children subject to care orders are more 'difficult' than those previously subject to approved school orders; it cannot show *how* and *why* these children are perceived as more 'difficult'.

For this reason we have taken, in our research, both a descriptive and an appreciative stance. The social workers concerned with the children (68 in all)* were routinely interviewed by us at each key event (such as a change placement) and at each key activity (such as reviews and case conferences). We also observed case conferences and review meetings. In this way, the description of 'what happened' as contained in the files can be better understood. Because of the limited nature of the sample, our intention is to generate hypotheses which may be later tested rather than to make definitive claims.

We have endeavoured to suspend the usual taken-for-granted assumptions concerning decision making in formal organizations. We are not, for example, concerned with whether decisions are 'rational' or 'non rational' (Weber, 1947), 'programmed' or 'unprogrammed', 'formal' or 'informal' (Etzioni, 1964). Neither are we concerned with whether decisions are 'good' or 'bad', 'right' or 'wrong',

---

*One further social worker refused to take part in the research and one case remained unallocated throughout the research period.

'professional' or 'unprofessional'. Rather we are attempting the more limited task of inquiring into the practices which social workers employ in sustaining the 'sense' that their own and others' conduct *is* decision making. As such, the central theme of our inquiry is to identify those issues which the actors themselves use when accounting for a decision and the meaning which these issues have (*see* Zimmerman, 1971). As Bittner (1974) has written about organizations in general:

> If one suspends the presumptive notion that a rational organizational scheme is a normative idealization with a simple import, i.e. demanding literally what it says it demands; and if one views a rational organizational scheme without information about what it is ostensibly meant to be, then it emerges *as a generalised formula to which all sorts of problems can be brought for solution.* In this sense there is no telling what determinations a formal organizational scheme contains prior to the time that questions are actually and seriously addressed to it. (Emphasis in original.)

This approach to the investigation of decision making within organizations is, of course, not unique. In the sphere of criminal justice research, the works of Sudnow (1967), Sachs (1972), Piliavin and Briar (1964) and Emerson (1969) stand as well-known examples. More particularly with respect to children, Cicourel's 'Social Organization of Juvenile Justice' (1976) depicts in great detail how the perspectives of juvenile justice personnel become authoritative accounts of 'what happened' and that decisions are 'produced' in accordance with these accounts. By revealing how information is assembled and 'made sense of', Cicourel shows how the mere dictionary reading of the language categories used by the actors is insufficient to an understanding of the process involved. He writes:

> The various expressions used by the police, probation and school officials for depicting juveniles do not depend for their meaning on some dictionary or literal interpretation of lexical items, but require an open texture of what 'anyone knows' and assumes 'others know' (1976).

This taken-for-granted background knowledge has to be exposed before a comprehensive understanding of the processes involved can be made.

In the area of social work, the recent work by Rees (1978) provides a useful illustration of what may be gained by adopting a naturalistic stance. By making the content of social work problematic, Rees shows how social workers make sense of a world which continually presents its participants with 'problems' which have to be resolved. Rees traces how 'problems' in social work are conceptualised, are evaluated in terms of work priorities and are then translated into practice. In addition, Rees looks at the world of the clients to ascertain not only how the service they receive is seen, but also how the clients shape and sustain how social workers see their world. In this way, Rees has argued that 'the concept of "treatment" can be robbed of its pretentiousness if the activities which are gathered under this label are defined' (1978).

In a similar vein but with rather more eclectic concerns is the recent survey of social work practice by Stevenson *et al* (1978). In particular, the work of Elizabeth Browne on social work activities uses practitioners' accounts to analyse how the various agency tasks are performed. Unlike Rees, however, Browne is far more concerned to contrast the accounts she collected against the assumed meta-structure of social work theory. Hence throughout her work there is an evaluative posture which implies that 'if only' the variables of social work education and agency organization could be changed then the perspectives of practitioners and theorists would be congruent. Whether or not this is so, we would argue, requires investigation in its own right.

Finally, there is a growing body of research which has made use of these methodological dictates to produce detailed accounts of social workers' ideologies with particular groups of clients in particular organizational settings (*see*, for example, Smith and Harris, 1972; May and Smith, 1978, 1979). Especially useful in this area is the work of Pauline Hardiker on the ideologies of probation officers (1977, 1979). By describing how these ideologies are put into practice, she has shown that our common taken-for-granted assumptions about how 'problems' are perceived by social welfare professionals is over-simplified. She writes:

> Treatment model assumptions about crime might constitute part of social work ideologies . . . however, (this) statement tells very little about . . . actual practices. (T)reatment orientations need to be considered in relation to the organizational context in which they work and this includes offences, offenders, their own agencies and the courts. Ideologies appear to be mediated by the exigencies of practice, and this may be one reason why notions about 'responsibility' and 'treatment' appear to exist side by side in social work. Once we examine the context in which social workers practise, it seems we can no longer argue that they go around applying a seductive casework model in a blind and global way (1977).

In approaching our present subject matter, we have treated as 'problematic' the world of the social workers we interviewed and have, therefore, adopted the qualitative methodology of loosely structured interview and observation. As Filstead writes, such an approach:

> . . . allows the researcher to 'get close to the data', thereby developing the analytical, conceptual and categorical components of explanation from the data itself – rather than from the preconceived, rigidly structured and highly quantified techniques that pigeonhole the empirical social world into the operational definitions that the researcher has constructed (1970).

Clearly the choice of the themes which we have presented here is our own, but we hope that we have demonstrated the general nature of these themes by a generous use of quotations. Following Stevenson *et al* (1978) we have tried to avoid 'phoney' quantification. But where matters of interest have been raised which are atypical or idiosyncratic, these have occasionally been included (with the necessary caveats) to illustrate both the diversity of responses and the possibility of alternative accounts.

All of our interviews with social workers were taped and full transcripts of these were made. Each social worker was interviewed at least three times and each interview lasted at least three-quarters of an hour, usually longer. In addition, when unexpected events occurred, the social workers concerned were interviewed as soon as possible thereafter. The social workers in the sample routinely informed us of any new event. When a new social worker was allocated to a case, he was immediately interviewed to gain the impressions given to him of the case by the previous social worker. We also attended, where permitted, and this was the usual practice, assessment conferences, team meetings at which the case was discussed and *ad hoc* meetings which were arranged. Recordings were made of these discussions, or where this was not allowed, and this was unusual, written notes were made by the observer. We have not attempted to 'doctor' the transcripts. Hesitations, repetitions, tautologies and the like have been retained in the accounts used as examples of particular points to convey some of the atmosphere of uncertainty or self-assuredness which social workers had about the areas discussed.

In our presentation of the information we were concerned with developing and articulating what we call the social workers' 'general' ideology. Strauss *et al* used this term in their studies of professional actors in the following way:

> Any body of systematically related beliefs held by a group of people, providing that the system of beliefs is sufficiently basic to the groups way of life (1964).

In relation to social work, this concept was recently elaborated on by Stuart Rees. He writes:

> 'Ideology' refers to interconnected sets of ideas which were incorporated into social workers' simplified and convenient interpretations of aspects of their occupations . . . Social workers' general ideology manifested beliefs and values which enabled the group to make sense of their work (1978).

But, to be true to the phenomenon, these ideologies must be set within the occasions of their use, what Hardiker has called 'the exigencies of practice' (1977). Hence we are concerned to show not only how social workers construct the routine, mundane, non-problematic realm of decision making but also how their assumptions and expectations in particular cases may be thwarted and the consequences this can produce. Our concern, therefore, is to determine what a 'competent' social work decision is. By 'competent' we mean, following Zimmerman, 'the members' practiced grasp of what particular actions are necessary on a given occasion to provide the production of a "normal" state of affairs' (1971). Where issues of social work theory are raised in practice, they are also discussed.

Our overall purpose in this research is to generate hypotheses; the validity of our account is a matter for further exploration. In order to satisfy ourselves of the validity of our account we gave a verbal report to each of the social workers in the sample after our last interview with them. This was supplemented later with a paper which they were asked to comment on. The widespread acceptance of the themes in that paper makes us feel that, for this sample at least, our analysis is an accurate representation of their decision-making. As to the reliability of our account, this too must ultimately be tested by research in other areas with other social workers. Nevertheless, the fact that we interviewed social workers from different offices in the same local authority as well as social workers from different local authorities gives some weight to our findings: the concepts used and the problems identified were similar, whatever their individual setting.

1

Offenders in Care

There has been very little research on children committed to care since the implementation of the Children and Young Persons Act of 1969 and yet, as we mentioned in the previous chapter, certain firm impressions exist. This project set out to examine some of these beliefs and this chapter describes those children who came into the care of the Inner London boroughs on offence grounds between 1 November, 1978 and 31 January, 1979. There were 79 such children and we have information on all but one, though some limited information on this child was obtained from court records.

The care order replaced both the approved school order and the fit person order. It is, therefore, unrealistic to make exact comparisons with pre-1971 data and so we have done this rarely. Generally one would expect children subject to a care order to be younger and less delinquent than those subject to approved school orders but to be older and more delinquent than those subject to a fit person orders (*see*, for example, Hoghughi, 1973).

The most significant study of care orders since 1971 is Cawson's unpublished research carried out for the D.H.S.S. A national survey of children in care during July, 1975 was compiled by postal questionnaire. In all, Cawson has information on 497 children. Not all authorities returned the questionnaires within the necessary time limit and consequently inner city children are underestimated in the sample. To some extent, therefore, this study complements Cawson's as it covers only inner city children. Wherever possible we have compared our data with that of Cawson. Tables which provide a full account of the information collected are available from the authors; a few are inserted in the appendix. The discussion which follows provides a summary of their main features.

Of the 79 children in our sample 68 (86%) were male and 11 (14%) were female. All but one of the females were black compared with less than a third of the boys. Half of the children were in the 13–15 age group. Only 8% were between 10 and 12 and a further 11% were between 16 and 17. One third of the sample lived with both natural parents.

As one would expect, the majority of the offences committed were offences against property (57%). The next most common category of offence was taking and driving away and related traffic offences (20%). Violent offences account for only 6% and sex offences for 3%. Although the method of recording crime in the Annual Criminal Statistics has changed considerably since 1972, we can make some very general comparisons between our sample and some earlier samples of approved school boys. It seems that taking and driving away and road traffic offences figure more commonly now than previously as do offences concerning criminal damage (*cf* Field *et al*, 1971 and Millham *et al*, 1975). Another interesting difference is an apparent change in peer group involvement in crime. Of our sample, 66% (based on 71 children for whom such information was available) committed their offences on their own compared with only 17% of Millham's approved school boy sample.

One of the surprising factors to emerge from this project was the relative lack of criminal sophistication in the sample: 73% had no record of having been given a police caution prior to the imposition of the care order. The actual figure may, of course, be lower as not all cautions may have been recorded, but two-thirds of Cawson's national survey had similarly not been cautioned. Furthermore, 45% of our sample were given a care order on their first appearance in court. This is considerably higher than Cawson's national figure of 31% and than figures on approved schools boys. Millham, for example, found that only 10% of his approved school had no previous record and two-thirds of Hoghughi's 1969–72 sample had experienced more than three court appearances. This trend towards early intervention is, of course, consistent with the social work ideology underlying the 1969 Act. Care orders seem frequently to be used as first as opposed to last resorts. One might have expected them to be imposed only after the imposition of nominal and supervision penalties, that is after a third court appearance. But only 27% of our sample had some previous experience of supervision; 45% had been fined and 18% had been given attendance centre orders.

It is difficult to discern clear patterns but two factors seem to distinguish these first time care order children from the rest of the sample: 46% of them had been known to the social services department for less than 12 months (compared with only 19% of the other children) and the parents of 51% of them had requested the imposition of the order (again compared with 18% of the other children).

Few of the children (12) had no previous care experience: 15 (12%) children had previously been or were subject to care orders at the time the current order was imposed (this is similar to Cawson's figure of 14%) and 16 had been in care under the provisions of the 1948 Children Act (that is, they had been placed voluntarily into care by their parents). On the other hand, more than half of those who had experienced care before the order had been the subject of interim care orders or had been remanded in care.

When the care order was made, relatively few children were actually living at home with their parents (27%). The comparable figure in Cawson's survey was 53%. This suggests that London children are more frequently remanded in care than children in other parts of the country although Cawson's research indicates that this is not because London children are more delinquent. The factors which appear to influence place of remand are unclear. The most common placement prior to the imposition of the care order was an observation and assessment centre (43%).

Immediately on the making of the care order, 25 children changed their placements. Half of these went directly into observation and assessment facilities. This meant that once the care order was made, 48% of the children were in observation and assessment centres. Only 8% were home on placement and a further 19% were at home awaiting placements. This is quite different from the stereotypical picture of the child in care presented by the Magistrates' Association (*see supra*: 1), but is fully in keeping with other research. Cawson, for example, found that two-thirds of her sample were placed in a residential institution of some kind on the day of the care order.

Previous delinquency showed no consistent relationship with type of placement. Indeed, our research confirms Cawson's view that there is a logical picture at the extremes: persistent offenders are rarely placed at home; first offenders are commonly placed at home. But by far the largest group was in the middle for whom no such predictions can be made.

The length of our follow up period was limited (6 months) but we can comment on two areas of general importance: subsequent offending and changes in placement. Again we will compare our findings with Cawson's, but a note of caution must be entered. Cawson extended her original 6 month follow up period to 9 months in order to increase the number of children who were placed after a period in an observation and assessment centre.

Further offences (21 in all) within 6 months of the care order were committed by 17 (22%) of the 79 children (36% of Cawson's sample had re-offended). Some 11 re-offended only after the care order; 6 had re-offended both before and after the care order. Generally, in the former group just under half were at home on placement (or in lodgings) and just over half were awaiting residential placement or were already placed there (albeit they were absconding or on leave at the time of the subsequent offences). In the latter group, on the other hand, all had been placed residentially or were absconding. Although the numbers we are discussing are very small, they do go some way towards questioning the view that it is *children placed at home* who commit further offences and that residential care orders would resolve the problem of re-offending.

Cawson's research confirms these impressions. The majority

of re-offenders in her sample were children already in residential care or absconding from it. This may, of course, be accounted for by the fact that such children are already 'high risk' children. It is now well documented that a previous record is a good indicator of subsequent delinquency (West and Farrington, 1973).

Cawson's research indicated that the sentencing of first time re-offenders was largely non-custodial and that for second time re-offenders the balance slightly altered. Our figures are too small to allow comment on this but placement at the time of re-offending and whether or not the offence pre-dates the care order both seem to be relevant factors in the magistrates' decision making. Those who re-offended before the care order was imposed but who were dealt with subsequently tended to be given minor penalties: fines and conditional discharges. (There was only one exception to this.) Those who subsequently offended and who were either placed at home or in residential establishments were also dealt with in this way. (Cawson found that those placed at home were dealt with more leniently than those placed in residential establishments.) On the other hand, those who re-offended after the care order was imposed and who were currently absconding from a residential placement were dealt with harshly: detention centre and borstal.

During the 6 month period, 78 children (one child had his care order rescinded within the 6 months' period) had a total of 161 placements. While 37% had only one placement, 6% had 5 or more. (The corresponding figures for Cawson's research are 19% and 9%. The difference is probably accounted for by the different follow-up periods.) On the day of their committal 72% of the children returned to the same type of placement as that in which they had spent the previous night. Only 25 children changed their placement when the care order was made: one child went from an assessment centre into lodgings, 2 children absconded from the juvenile court, 3 went from a residential establishment to their parents home; one child went from a residential establishment to his parents' home: one child went from assessment centre to C.H.E; one was moved from his parents to a special school; 5 children (2 from their parents and 3 from assessment centres) were placed in children's homes; and 12 went into observation and assessment facilities (6 from their parents, 3 from children's homes and 3 from remands in care). In all, 9 children left their home to go into residential placement.

During the 6 months of the study 53 children (68%) spent some time in an observation and assessment centre. The longest stay was the full six months; the shortest was one day. The most common time period for the sample to have spent in observation and assessment was the full 6 months. In all, 11 children (14% of the example) remained there for the full six months. On the imposition of the care order, 37 of the children (48%) were placed in observation and assessment centres immediately. However, 10 children (13%) of the sample, entered an assessment centre only when their previous placement broke down. Of these 7 had been in children's home or hostels; 3 had been in their own home. Of the sample, 37% had their longest placement in observation and assessment centres.

The children who went to assessment centres as their first placements were likely to spend a long period there. After one month, only 22% had been placed; 56% stayed more than three months. In the former system, it was usual for approved school boys to spend one month in classifying centres. These long periods of assessment may indicate that the assessment process requires investigation. On the other hand, almost a third (29%) had no assessment placement during the period. None of these children were assessed non-residentially and only 10 had been assessed prior to the care order. This raises a question about why the care order was sought (or imposed) in the first instance. It was rare in our sample (3% compared with Cawson's figure of 8%) for a child to have more than one assessment placement.

At least once during the follow up for reasons other than holidays and visits, 36% of the sample returned home. After a period of observation and assessment 18 (22%) children were placed at home directly or as the desired placement. Although there was no significant association between home placement and previous delinquency, there was a trend in that direction. Compared with 37% of those who were placed elsewhere, 11 (61%) had been given a care order on their first appearance in court. (Cawson also found that children placed at home were no more serious offenders than those placed in residential care.) If we take all the periods spent at home, however, about half of these were at home awaiting placement. This indicates, to some extent, the inadequacy of current resources. Only 28% of those placed at home came from single parent families. There was, however, no significant association between placement and family structure, though again there was a trend in that direction.

During the 6 months following the care order, 31 children (40% of the sample) had a residential placement (other than a C.H.E.): children's home (17), hostel (11), special school or boarding school (4). (One child had two such placements.) Of these children 58 were first offenders and this seems to have been significant in the decision to place them there. With respect to C.H.E. placement, only 23% of the children so placed (5 out of 22) were first offenders and there was a significant relationship between C.H.E. placement and previous delinquency. Family structure, on the other hand, did not seem a significant factor: about half of the children in each category came from single parent families.

Thirteen children had 14 'breakdowns' or premature terminations of their placements. Five of these 'breakdowns' occurred while the child was placed at home as the desired placement. In two of these cases, the child committed further delinquent acts. One was then placed in an observation and assessment centre prior to a court hearing and the other was remanded by the juvenile court on an 'unruly certificate'. The remaining breakdowns in this category were said to be due to parental inability to cope. Two of these children were then placed in observation and assessment centres; the third was placed in a children's home.

Nine of the breakdowns occurred while the child was in a

residential placement. Four breakdowns were due to the child being removed by order of a juvenile court (2 children were remitted to the Crown Court and were eventually sentenced to borstal and one child had two separate spells in a detention centre) after the commission of subsequent offences. Three breakdowns were due to the children being too disruptive for children's homes. All of these were then placed in observation and assessment centres. One breakdown involved the premature closedown of a hostel; this child was then placed at home to await further placement. And the final breakdown was a child who was described as too disruptive for a special school. He subsequently ran away and committed offences while absconding. He was placed in a hostel over the weekend and then returned home to await his court hearing as the social worker said that he did not know what else to do. This child was subsequently given a detention centre order by the court.

At the end of the research period, 20 children were in community homes with education on the premises, 18 were in other residential establishments and 15 children were still in the observation and assessment centres. Whereas 11 children were at home as a placement, only 4 were at home awaiting placement. 4 boys were in either detention centre or borstal.

In trying to understand placements we examined a number of factors: age, family structure, previous record etc. As with other research in this area (Cawson, 1978; May 1977 and 1978) no significant relationships were found and we are forced to agree with May that 'the choice of placement type for each youngster is presumably made on subtler grounds than those available for study'. The fact that it is difficult for outsiders to 'make sense' of placement decisions by reference to factors which might appear related underlies the importance of other chapters of this study.

2

What Type of Case is This?

In order to understand how social workers made their decisions we did not assume that social services departments respond in some rational or bureaucratic way to cases. In deciding whether or not a problem exists, the nature of a particular problem and the appropriate response to it, social workers must make choices. As with many other areas of professional judgement, these choices go largely unstructured. Allowing discretion is in some ways the essence of a profession: the recognition that there is a service based on a body of esoteric knowledge of which this individual (doctor, lawyer, social worker or whoever) is a competent exponent (Adler and Asquith, 1981). Consequently, in understanding how discretion is exercised, that is, how decisions are made, we must look to how the actors *themselves* make sense of the issues they use when claiming to act as competent professionals.

In social work in particular, not all cases referred to a social services department are seen as 'problems' and not all 'problems' are dealt with in the same way (though they may share legal or other categorisation). The social worker *chooses* his cases. As Rees writes:

Given most social workers' dependence on only a few administrative and legal guide-lines and their assumption that resources are always in short supply, the practice of social work should be depicted by the notion of caring for only certain categories of people and problems rather than by the more common but uncritical dramatisations of their profession's virtues in caring for all (1978).

In this chapter we describe how social workers decide what the 'real issues' are in care order cases. The relationship between these real issues and the ostensible basis of the care order and the place of the order in the social worker's repertoire of professional skills shows how care orders are used as a resource for identifying pressing practical problems rather than as a remedy for them.

'It's a very mixed process as to how kids are taken into care'

The notion that social workers select their clients from a pool of potential clients was established early in our research. Not every application for help by a parent was treated, at least initially, as a 'real problem'. The following statement by a social worker illustrates this:

> The first referral was about June when John's parents came in saying they were having problems with him, basically because he was running away for fairly extended periods and that he was upsetting them. They seemed to be more upset because he was running away rather than why he was running away or whether he was O.K. when he ran away. We said that was bad news but there is little we can do about it. Come back if the problem persists; and they reappeared about a month later . . . I considered the problem pretty serious when they came back and this behaviour was still going on.

Though our research concerns children made the subject of a care order on offence grounds, the offence itself was often not the primary criterion in determining whether or not the child presented a real problem for the social worker. As one social worker put it:

> I really didn't think that the shop-lifting was important. I thought it was much more important that both places where the girl had been living were falling apart and that she couldn't live there. If they had just been shop-lifting offences or she had had some place to live and the shop-lifting offence had come up then I think that care would have to have been looked at much more carefully and we might not have decided to take her into care.

The main reasons were that we felt at that stage that we wanted to go straight through to a full care order. The situation at home seemed to have broken down. Mother appeared to have lost control of her son at home and there didn't seem to be any realistic possibility that her son could remain at home for very much longer. In fact, I wasn't aware of the offences at all. Owen told me that he had been in trouble with the police for a minor theft and that he was waiting to be charged. On the morning of the court hearing after the interim care order had been granted, Owen told me that the police were going to charge him with the burglary offence and that was the first time I became aware of the offences.

The request for a care order ostensibly on the grounds of a criminal offence, therefore, often had little to do with the social worker's belief as to the nature of the 'real problem'. The majority of the social workers, in fact, disregarded the child's delinquency as a focus of concern.

Well I had to see it mainly from the court's point of view in the sense that a child was involved in offending. But I wasn't only seeing it from the court's point of view. The delinquency, I just see that as a symptom rather than something to be cured, if you like, which is probably not the way the court sees it. I saw the delinquency as a symptom rather than a cause, so I was looking at it from a more broad angle if you like.

*   *   *

I would personally see the primary importance of the care order as that here is a kid who has been out of school for a long time and he's not receiving any education and the quality of controls and direction and guidance at home is very questionable and the care order is needed in order to establish him in a school and maintain him in a school and take some responsibility away from the mother who hasn't been able to discharge her responsibilities as a parent as well as she might. That is how I would see it, but the court were obviously also concerned about the offending and the fact that it is the third time he's been in court.

*   *   *

The magistrates nearly made a supervision order and a fine which is the more conventional way of dealing with this kind of situation, right. It had to be explained to them that we would not be able to get her into an assessment unit at Cumberlow Lodge because Middlesex Lodge won't do assessments for the Cumberlow catchment area, right, nor, I would like to explain, would Middlesex Lodge take her under any circumstances without an interim care order or a full care order, so I had to explain that to them, so we then got the care order.

The fact that the social workers (or their departments) had previously been involved with many of these children informally through previous family contact (see Appendix A: V) usually meant that a considerable amount of background knowledge could be taken for granted when determining the 'real problems' of the case. Frequently the offence merely compounded suspicions that there were in fact 'real problems'.

Marcus had never officially been involved with courts before and normally having a care order for a kid that had never been in court before would be frightening. But I think that in this particular case the lad had been involved in petty crime that has not come to the notice of the authorities and in a sense with the family background situation a care order is probably the best thing.

Moreover, the involvement of other agencies after the child had committed an offence seemed directly to influence the belief that 'something must be done.'

As soon as there is something like this, a criminal situation, the court's going to look at what to do in relation to these offences. Then, if you like, on balance you look at the family situation and you look at it in a slightly different way and I would say that, yes, between the time she was arrested and the time that it was apparent she was going to come up in court I suppose there is actually a change of emphasis on saying yes this child is better off, on balance, out of the family than in the family, which you were not willing to say before.

*   *   *

Obviously when the police did become involved suddenly the family situation became a lot more rocky inasmuch as mother was not going to accept Veronica stealing and getting into trouble. It was alright if she was stealing and nobody was rocking the boat but suddenly there were the police and that was bringing shame on

her as a mother and she increasingly said I want no more to do
with it.

*   *   *

As a result of a case conference that was held by the education
welfare officer who was working with him at the time we were
discussing whether to go to court to get a care order on grounds of
non-attendance. He hadn't been going to school for so long, but
then the criminal offence came up. When he smashed up this bus
shelter and the police became involved . . . it seemed pretty
evident that a care order was to be made at some stage so we
thought we might as well go to court and make it.

Consequently, many social workers talked of the child's
offence as being 'an excuse' for intervention which would not
have been possible had the incident not taken place.

I don't see him really as that much of a delinquent. The whole
thing was taken as a fairly fortuitous thing on my part to bring him
into care. I don't think that it was ever serious.

*   *   *

It wouldn't have come to our notice probably or we may not have
had grounds, unless, of course, the family brought him to us and
said 'well we can't cope with him, we want him taken into care', in
which case we would have received him into care under the '48
Act.

Social workers' assumptions that parents would not cooperate
with them or would not consent to voluntary forms of
intervention were also powerful motivating forces in choosing
statutory powers.

There was a lot of mixed feelings on the father's part about the
care order but I began to think it was good that I had it. I feel that
if I had remained on a voluntary basis I would have had
difficulties. If John had caused difficulties I don't know how the
father would have reacted. I think he has mixed feelings about the
children being in care.

*   *   *

We were sort of waiting for an opportunity to have some sort of powers over the children and the family. Obviously his Section 1 didn't work because mother also wanted him home and I had reached a point where it was quite forseeable that if he remained home any longer then the situation would just continue to deteriorate and he was in very bad trouble and then possibly reach a stage when very little could be done about it.

* * *

They are one of those families where there is no go. They don't answer the door half the time, the electricity is cut off, things like that, so they don't always open the door, and, in fact, we took a conscious decision not to intervene in this case, thinking that . . . you see he was in care before under Section 1 for about three years and she discharged him . . . well I made a few attempts to visit and didn't get anywhere at all, I don't think I ever saw the mother, I don't think she was ever in when I went, I mean I wrote letters, then I tried the surprise technique, no response. So with my senior, that we had at the time, we discussed it and decided that there was no point in going and wasting our time and we would just leave it with the knowledge that when something happened we would go for a court order.

Similarly, the assumption that supervision would not work or had previously been attempted without success (albeit informally and by other agencies) meant that social workers did not feel that formal supervision was necessary before applying for the care order. The notion of the care order as a sequential form of intervention which was preceded by other, less intensive, forms of work was not one commonly used by social workers. Only a small percentage of our sample had previously been the subject of supervision orders.

I don't think Ray would have been suitable for supervision. A lot of work has been done on the family not only by myself but also by youth detachment workers and E.W.O.s etc., and certainly Ray has gone to Youth Clubs for a week or two and then given up when he decided that he really didn't like it very much. So I don't think that supervision or intermediate treatment would have been suitable for him.

* * *

I think that it was the feeling that things were unworkable at home. I think that was the major criteria as opposed to supervising a child at home. Dad was basically saying I can't cope.

* * *

I have been seeing Paul, but then there was no supervision order, I have been seeing him individually, trying to do some preventive work while he was in the home situation which wasn't working at all. Another option we tried was having him for a short period on a voluntary care order and that hadn't worked because that didn't provide enough stability because it was a situation where he could go home at anytime and mother still had all the rights and it didn't provide him with the sorts of barriers that I think he needed. The other options were to work with the family which I have been doing for a number of years and there has been very little change. It has been a matter of . . . continual crisis intervention, so that didn't really seem to be a solution. So there were very few options left really.

* * *

On the basis that the educational welfare authorities had been involved with the family for well over twelve months and they had tried to offer help to the family and to the boy himself in the form of child guidance, special classes, counselling at home, and all of these were outrightly rejected by the child, and we didn't feel that a supervision order would carry very much weight. It wouldn't do very much with him.

* * *

The father is very angry at social services. He feels that they haven't done enough. He feels that the supervision order failed because social services didn't, in fact, supervise. But frankly a supervision order wouldn't have worked in this case ever because you can't in fact . . . someone supervising wouldn't have been able to resolve the particular difficulties in the home. There was no way that those difficulties were going to be resolved by a social worker going in week after week and trying to resolve what are now very acute difficulties, father and his wife.

Implicit in these accounts of the inapplicability of supervision is the belief that the *client* is the unsuitable party; the supervising agency is rarely seen as unsuitable, inflexible or wrong. In the case of Steven, the Child Guidance Clinic made an offer of family therapy in their first report. In its second report, which was sent to the court, there was reference to the further offences committed by Steven and the comment that the Clinic did not feel it could deal with the boy. When asked whether this was not rejecting on the part of the Clinic, the boy's social worker replied.

> No, they weren't rejecting. They were saying what they have to offer, or, if you aren't able to take up what we have to offer then we don't have anything else.

This means, of course, that the decreasing use of supervision orders in the juvenile courts since the passing of the 1969 Act (*see* Morris and Giller, 1978) should not solely be attributed to magistrates' sentencing policy. Supervision is frequently neglected by social workers themselves as an alternative response to their client's 'troubles'. In the words of one social worker:

> The supervison order seems to me to be a complete and utter loss; you don't really have any sort of real teeth.

The care order then is not seen as a cure for an agenda of problems mutually defined between the various agencies involved. As one social worker put it:

> Most social workers, including myself, have reservations about the effectiveness of a care order and we don't see them as being a magic solution to solving problems of this kid or many other kids for that matter.

Indeed, most social workers described the care order in terms which suggest that, at most, all that was being achieved was the formal recognition of a social problem:

> There's a large element in the fact that we needed to get more information . . . But also I am sure he needed to be in care in some sense.

* * *

B

A care order is necessary to get access to things, to put things in focus, you have to have a starting point.

Many social workers made this apparent to the court in the social enquiry reports which they prepared:

I was just trying to show the court what the home circumstances were and obviously there was some problem with Allan and that needed further investigation and for our purposes the only way we could achieve that investigation would be for the care order with assessment because of the breakdown of the previous attempts of child guidance and so on.

* * *

Over the past six months Oliver has been involved in a series of offences and this may reflect the abrupt changes in his life over the last few years. In the present circumstances, the Supervision Order that was made in September would not seem to give sufficient opportunity to this Department to make firm plans for Oliver's future. Therefore I would respectfully recommend that Care Order be made in respect of Oliver.

* * *

Paul's needs do appear to point towards a Care Order, although both the regional assessment centre and I are at a loss as to which type of placement could most appropriately meet the needs of Paul and given this I would respectfully suggest that the Court may feel that it would be appropriate to return Paul to the regional assessment centre for a full assessment, so that we can best judge which placement would best meet this boy's social and educational needs.

The care order provided the social worker also with latent power – a coercive power which *might* have to be used against the wishes of the child and his family.

A care order gives more scope for taking more responsibility, making a plan. It puts more onus on us to devise some sort of treatment plan. If it's just voluntary I think it's in limbo really. The expectation is that the kid is going home pretty soon . . .

* * *

. . . Well the only reason I took a care order over John was it was the only way to get him to a community home. For a start, it is very difficult to get him in under Section 1 of the 1948 Act, I think, partly because they can't keep the boys.

*　　*　　*

I think that if things had been left . . . we would have not been able to persuade the mother to either get him to school regularly, to keep him off the streets and keep him out of trouble. Neither would we have been able to persuade him to go away voluntarily somewhere.

*　　*　　*

I wasn't willing to go on Section 1 as it doesn't give me enough power to assess the child.

The care order, therefore, is a legal resource used to identify problems, not, of itself, to define what those problems are or how professional action should progress (*see also* Grace and Wilkinson, 1978)

Although the majority of children went through some sort of formal (residential) assessment after the care order was made, it was clear that the social workers themselves had already made a preliminary assessment of 'what type of case it was' even before the order was made. In essence, social workers must first evaluate 'the case' and construct a 'logical' plan for intervention before any formal decisions can be reached.

What type of case is this?

It is probably a minority of children who grow up without ever misbehaving in ways which may be contrary to the law. Frequently such behaviour is no more than an incident in the pattern of a child's normal development. But sometimes it is a response to unsatisfactory family or social circumstances, a result of boredom in and out of school, an indication of maladjustment or immaturity or a symptom of a deviant, damaged or abnormal personality (Home Office, 1968).

This quotation from the White Paper 'Children in Trouble' encapsulates the notion that not all crime represents 'real trouble'. Not all delinquency needs the attention of social welfare professionals; as many sociologists of deviance have pointed out, were it otherwise the machinery of criminal justice would quickly come to a grinding halt (*see* Cicourel, 1976). Social workers, therefore, are sensitised to look for 'real trouble'. This may be found within the child's family, personality or behaviour. As we have shown, it is only in limited situations that the child's offence is the primary reason for intervention and that the ascription of 'real delinquent' is made out on that basis alone. The offence *per se* provides no sure guide for action and so has to be interpreted through the background and character of the child and his family (*cf* Matza, 1964, and Emerson, 1969). As one social worker put it:

> I mean, clearly I would feel that if a member of a family is committing some offences there must be some difficulties within the family or the culture within which they operate, that is one which is geared to the delinquent activity.

Our interviews suggest that, where the offence can be explained by notions of 'family trouble', then it will pale into insignificance. One social worker, for example, when asked about the reason for the care order, catalogued in great detail the mother's marriage breakdown, the consequential housing problems and the child's school refusal. After ten minutes on these issues, the social worker was asked how the offence fitted into this:

> The offence took place when all this was going on . . . it seemed to me to be all part of the same thing of being an especially confusing situation for Paul. He isn't able to explain anything. At the same time as he couldn't explain why he isn't going to school or didn't want to think about it, he also didn't want to think or explain about the offence. But, in fact, when you look at the offence it is a very minor thing. It involved a garage attendant. He was kind of helping out there on Saturday morning or something like that and there was £10 lying around on a pay packet, lying around on the table and he took the £10. Well he actually gave £8 of that back, so the offence is actually only stealing £2. But the thinking there was tied in with the fact, with the idea of taking the care proceedings anyway because . . . well to back track . . . I was liaising quite

closely with the education welfare about it and our joint thinking on it was that it seemed quite clear that the situation at home for Paul was too much for him, it just wasn't right and he was just getting worse. The school attendance and the offences were all tied up with it. What was obvious was that he did need to be removed from the home and at the same time that is what he had been asking for all along.

The offence became subsumed into the 'family troubles'. The social worker, by minimising the significance of the offence, allowed alternative explanations to dominate his reading of the case.

A similar picture emerged in Steven's case. Steven is a 14 year old boy who was charged on his first appearance in the juvenile court with six counts of burglary and seven other offences were taken into consideration. The social worker thought that this level of delinquency was 'unusual in a lad of his age' and recommended that a care order be made in order to see what the problem was. Soon after the order was made, however, the social worker began to ignore the offences and concentrated on what was seen to be the 'real trouble': Steven's parents.

Well I suppose I don't feel myself that kids behave in that way without there being some problems for them, either within the family, within the school or in other places and there didn't seem to be that much problem with the school for him and I felt having met his mother and father there was a problem.

The influence of this assumption that 'something was wrong in the home' is well documented (*see* Cicourel, 1976; Emerson, 1969) and was frequently referred to by the social workers interviewed by us. But, as the above quotation illustrates, social workers' descriptions of their work do not suggest that practice is drawn from specific theoretical perspectives. According to Browne, 'many of the experienced workers were accustomed to working mainly at an intuitive level' (1978), Barry's social worker, when asked how the conclusion was made that Barry's offences were related to a conflict with his father, replied:

Well it's circumstantial in a sense, you know, there's a lot of supposition really. You listen to what was said . . . the mother presented a whole picture of a marriage which was a total disaster, alcoholism, aggression, violence, the whole thing. She's had two other fairly stable relationships and these had ended similarly, they had been disasters. I don't know it's a question of gut feeling I suppose. It's not terribly professional but you get a feeling and also there was the woman's manner. When she was with me there was a sort of edginess, a restlessness and it just occurred to me that if this is her normal manner or at least when she's unable or feeling herself to be unable to cope, to manage, I would think she probably doesn't contribute much to the stability of a relationship that there would be a lot of unease and my guess is that Barry might well have been responding in a way that her husband had . . .

Indeed, many of the social workers we interviewed seemed ill at ease when the conversation moved towards theory:

I could bring out some wishy-washy theory that John needs a break from the family and his parents are not able to let him go. John has slipped down the path of opting out and it's the one way of showing he's different, a sort of teenage identity thing . . . it's all theory really.

*   *   *

Steven was pushing his mother around as, this might be a bit theoretical, but as he had seen his father relating to this mother. This was his experience of life with his parents, how the male figure was always bullying, pushing, shouting, screaming. His behaviour was totally consistent with his experience of that.

*   *   *

Possibly underneath all the dependency and his fears of being separate from mum and everything he's going through a normal adolescent need to break away and, this is all out of the top of my head, but maybe, but I haven't thought around it, and maybe the offences were providing a function in the sense that they were hitting out at mum and their relationship, proving himself in his own right in a way.

Although these attempts at theoretical analysis seem confused and incoherent it would be wrong to assume that they did not aid the social worker's understanding of the case. But to assume theory and practice to be precisely 'worked out' presumes that social workers approach their cases in an a-contextual manner; this is not so. Browne also found this:

> There was evidence that social workers used concepts from sociology, social and individual psychology to understand clients and their difficulties. But there was less evidence that these concepts had been assimilated into an integral system to guide practice (1978).

The case of Robert, a 15 year old boy who had been recently excluded from his parental home, illustrates this further. During an interview with the mother, the social worker had obtained a detailed history of the boy:

> The mother told me that from a very early age the boy had smeared faeces and up to the age of four-and-a-half he had been doing things like pulling the bed away from the wall and excreting down the back of the bed. She claimed this behaviour stopped, but later told me that he started stealing from a lodger that they had at that time and from themselves soon after. She made no connection between these two incidents. Strictly on a reality base the kid was living in lift shafts on an estate with some kids on the estate who were quite expert at breaking into parking meters. Given those circumstances the kid might well steal anyway . . . I am not prepared to come down on one side or the other, just try and put everything into context. Some of these problems stem right back from early on, which has led to his exclusion from the family, that is within the family. What actually happens when he goes out the front door, there's also his peers and other things going on as well.

Theory is not used in a way which makes the inexplicable explicable but rather as a resource to bolster a previously ascertained pragmatic understanding of the case. It is only when one analyses the construction of those pragmatic assumptions that the use of theory becomes clear (*see also* Garfinkel, 1974 and Curnock and Hardiker, 1979).

Sense cannot be made of the remarks made by social workers about their theoretical understanding of their clients' problems without knowing something about the typical case or the typical purpose of the use of such theories. For example, 59% of the children in our sample were made the subject of care orders at their first or second appearance in court. In the majority of these cases, the social workers said that the use of the care order in this way was atypical:

> I think it's untypical really. I don't see him basically as being a delinquent kid. I don't know what the proportions are but certainly over 50% of the kids who come into care for that sort of reason are probably delinquent. With Steven, I feel that his delinquency is very much related to his relationship problem and it's not always as clear as that with the other kids.

> *   *   *

> I don't think that Veronica is typical in terms of offences and the care order in that this was her first time in court although she had been cautioned before and I feel that it's only because there were very very different reasons within the family set-up that made me feel we should go for a care order.

> *   *   *

> In my experience not very typical because he is much younger than most of the ones who have come into care for committing offences. It is a very minor offence, a first offence, and those two reasons, mainly whilst I have been a social worker, it is fairly untypical.

As to the typical case:

> Normally there are three or so offences, or seven or eight. I would say a normal pattern of a care order for a kid who is committing criminal offences is that it starts off as fairly minor when the kid is twelve or so . . . It's much more normal to look at the situation and say this is the kid's first offence hopefully he is not going to re-offend. There's conditional discharge and then there's fines and then there's deferred sentences and then you're going to have attendance centre order and then, eventually, if the kid's still offending and not responding to anything then you might start thinking well we're going to have to try removing the kid from the family situation and, therefore, recommend a care order or the

Bench take it upon themselves and say we really think there has been quite enough of this and want this person on a care order.

*   *   *

The typical case would be a case of a kid who's committed a number of offences, who, say on the first offence, got a conditional discharge, on the second offence got a fine and supervision order, a progression certainly. I would see the care order coming after a progression of things. Whether detention centre comes before a care order or after, I am not sure, but certainly a progressive kind of thing.

Implicit in these statements is the belief that early intervention provides the social worker with increased scope for preventing matters from becoming 'worse'. For example:

I think that the care order was right at the point that he had got to, given that he was involved in other offences as well, that he would have gone and got worse and into worse trouble, and it has provided a sort of, you know, some sort of full stop. It provided the opportunity to actually remove him and I think that he wouldn't have gone if there was a care order, and I don't think voluntarily he would have gone. It seems to me that he is very attached to home and in a lot of ways if I said 'alright you can go home now' he would in fact go, I think.

The offence then is seen primarily as symptomatic of wider problems. In essence, the 'medical model' of crime causation is being utilised. May (1971) has summarised the assumptions of this model as follows:

(1) Explanations of delinquency are to be found in the behaviour and motivational systems of delinquents and not the law and its administration.

(2) In some identifiable way delinquents are different from non-delinquents.

(3) The delinquent is constrained and cannot ultimately be held responsible for his actions.

(4) Delinquent behaviour *per se* is not the real problem; it is the presenting symptom that draws attention to more intractable disorder.

These assumptions underlie the 1969 Children and Young Persons Act which provided the structural legitimation of this professional concern. Social workers must inquire into the nature of the presenting offence to understand the child's real needs. Like his probation officer counterpart, the social worker looks 'for factors which make for less rational and more determined behaviour' (Hardiker and Webb, 1979). In 'decoding' the world of the child, social workers test out their theories within the particular context of the case before them. Hence theories are context-oriented, opaque, and, in Zimmerman's terms, 'practical accomplishments' (1974) which are called in aid to identify the presence and nature of 'real problems'. Social workers' accounts of the theoretical underpinning of the child's troubles reflect these taken-for-granted assumptions of the status of the case. The more closely the case can be interpreted as reflecting these treatment assumptions, the greater the likelihood that the case will be seen as a 'care case' and the child's delinquency will not be a specific area of concern. Conversely, the more the case is seen as deviating from this the greater the likelihood that the child's delinquency will become the specific area of concern. But before such a decision can be made, the social worker must adopt, again in Zimmerman's terms, 'the investigative stance' to the circumstances before him.

A crucial feature in the social worker's interpretation of the case is the ease with which a genealogy of problems can be constructed:

Obviously the whole thing is linked up with the family dynamics. A lot of it has to do with mother's perception of herself as a mother and of what she can do and could do for her children. It is also to do with her way of controlling the children, the inconsistencies of that method. For instance, she was brought up in a children's home because she had psoriasis and so from about two to fifteen she spent her childhood in hospitals and children's homes and was visited about half a dozen times by her parents. A couple of other brothers spent a long time in children's homes as well. So, therefore, she always tried to make up to the children for what she missed out on, and also she has tried to make up for the children's father leaving them when they were very young. So the home is absolutely superbly decorated and furnished. It's a housing association property. Mum does absolutely everything in the house. She paints, wallpapers, does the woodwork, anything she can do she does. And she gives the children everything she possibly can in material terms. Their clothing is superb, she gets everything from secondhand stalls, 20 or 25p, washes it, so they are always very neatly dressed, but really what she finds very difficult to give them is to give them affection and love and also any sort of consistency of care. She finds it very difficult to tell them off because she feels then that they see her as the bad sort of person. It has been difficult taking on the role of mother and father and being the person who tells the child off and also being the person who gives them sort of love and affection, and she has never really been able to come to terms with that. Many of the offences, in fact, that the children have committed have been against her. She keeps her purse under the bed because otherwise they would steal it. She can't leave any money in the house because they would take it, the punishment she gives isn't consistent. At one time she might keep them in, for a couple of days perhaps; the next time she will let them out. The children are . . . in some ways the children are testing her out to see what she will do, and also there are other things like she gives to them in material terms, they take from her in that way, in the same sort of way. One of the things that she has is this thing of controlling and the sort of morals that she gives the children, to the children, which are obviously inconsistent. So on the one hand she is saying 'Don't do it'. But yet she is saying 'O.K. we'll forget about it'. And so really the children haven't picked up throughout their lives any real sense of what is right and wrong.

Gary's social worker accounted for his delinquency in a similar way:

Gary was a child that was conceived before his parents were married. They were both very young and they had to get married because of the pregnancy. And I think that since that time there has been a lot of pressure on Gary because he wasn't wanted. They separate, come together, and since my involvement Gary had often been related to be very like father, so I think mother has got the identity of the two very mixed up. So he has got very tied in with the feelings that she has got towards her husband. Both sides have had affairs with considerable rowings.

The following account shows the same process of construction.

The boy had a very difficult beginning because he was born in England and was sent back to Jamaica when he was two, and he lived in Jamaica when he was two to six and put down roots there and was very fond of an aunt and a granny who brought him up, and didn't want to come back to England and never settled down when he was in England as the other children did, and I didn't think he ever really looked on his mother as mother, basically, so he had a bad start.

Histories of recent death or divorce, homelessness, poverty and the like clearly provided social workers with ready indicators of 'family problems'. But even where 'family problems' were not apparent, social workers seemed often to persist in their inquiries until some connection appeared. In Brian's case, for example, the social worker could find no explanation why the boy who came from 'a very united sort of family' would not attend school. By chance, the social worker discovered that Brian's parents could not read or write and that they had rejected school. For the social worker this proved sufficient explanation:

> When we had discussed that his parents had both had bad school experiences, it then emerged that his mother when telling him to go to school was really identifying with his fear of school and wasn't making him go at all. If she could say to him without ambivalence that he must go to school then he would have gone. In fact, she shares his worry about his failure. She is very ambitious for him and fears that he is going to fail and, therefore, he doesn't go and I think that is the crux of the problem.

In other cases, even less tangible indicators were relied upon. In Steven's case, for example, the social worker explained that she had established that the 'real problem' was the boy's parents soon after meeting them for the first time:

> The mother and father are very anxious and talked non-stop throughout the initial interview and were obviously very anxious to put the blame on Steven and not to look at anything else other than Steven. On meeting Steven, I felt that he wanted to take the blame rather than look at the family as well but he was obviously very anxious about anyone working with the family.

The discovery of a genealogy of 'problems' does not mean that alternative motivational accounts of the child's behaviour are ignored. But the extent to which alternative explanatory frameworks are sought depends on the success which social workers have when they use 'treatment model' assumptions. Hence factors which challenge the treatment model are often reinterpreted, deemphasised or recontextualised. The following example illustrates this relationship:

This is an area, Ladbroke Grove, where there is a lot of . . . no there is a cultural . . . of black/white difficulties, tensions, and I am sure that there is much more pressure upon teenagers in this area with regard to that cultural stress than possibly any other group in the population, and that has all sorts of little things to do with it, and there are lots of West Indian adolescents that are at odds with their parents, families, who feel very alienated from their own West Indian cultural backgrounds, at the same time completely alienated from what on earth is going on educationally here and employment possibilities, and that sort of thing. So there is all of that, and also the distress consequently that arises with the police and various other agencies in the area. And I think that is an important cultural background in which you can see Oliver's plight and all the kids who have been involved in this sort of major sort of robbery offence. There is a lot of drifting consequently. Teenagers don't expect to be at home very much, or have very sort of tight constraints placed on them by their parents. If they do, it is a very polarised situation. They will just react massively to the sort of tight constraints that very often West Indian older parents will place upon their kids and so they will stay out and they will squat, so they won't work regularly and they will join 'rastafarians' and all sorts of things. And I bet there are quite a few kids in Oliver's little gang of friends for whom that is sort of a fairly typical lifestyle. For Oliver more specifically, he has grown up in a background of no father figure, didn't know his father at all. In fact, notably, his surname is his mother's maiden name. His older sister Sandra knows of hers and hasn't seen him for about ten years, and her surname again is different from mother's, so there is that. Also as far as I can see from our records the mother has had a difficulty with mental illness that goes back nine years now, which is a substantial part of Oliver's life, that takes him back to six or so. He has never really known a mother who is consistently stable and healthy, and that has inevitably meant that he has come into care on occasions in the past, not particularly lengthy ones but nonetheless there have been interruptions. I think that that must reflect itself on general trauma of their life which is punctuated by family instability and not quite knowing where you are going to spend the next few months.

As this quotation makes clear, sociological explanations for the child's behaviour sometimes contradict or, at least, question the social worker's reliance on psychological frameworks. But such reinterpretations of the child's role, for example by ignoring the offence or seeing the child as a 'follower' rather than a 'leader', means that these sociological accounts are coopted into an overall deterministic framework. We discuss later in this chapter the interrelationship between sociological and psychological accounts.

This process whereby the family emerges as the basic unit of 'need' has been well documented by other researchers who have examined social workers' ideologies (*see* Smith and Harris, 1972; Hardiker, 1977; Hardiker and Webb, 1979; Browne, 1978). There remains to be discussed a minority of cases in which intervention is directed towards the child because of his delinquency. Here the child and not the family becomes the focus of the social worker's concern. Consequently an ideology of individual need emerges and with it the assumption that the child is a 'real delinquent'. Three types of accounts lead social workers to interpret cases in this way.

First, there are those situations in which the child is seen as the product of a family whose influence is totally negative. As a result the child himself is seen to have 'problems' which are beyond any remedy the social worker can provide. An example of such a child is Gary. His social worker summarised the position in the following manner:

The family are just a bunch of crooks really. They're all into stealing and fencing and Gary's been brought up in that way. He's just a socially conditioned, amoral delinquent and there's precious little I can do about it.

Martin's social worker saw the case in a similar way:

I don't think that it is in the least surprising that he got into trouble, taking into account that he hasn't been to school, he has had lots of time on his hands. Mum's sometimes . . . well I think mum's position generally is to not directly condone what the boys were doing but to excuse it or give reasons for it . . . certainly it could be seen as a fairly amoral sort of background in which to grow up and so it is hardly surprising that they have got into trouble.

Alternatively, the child's delinquency may be seen as a product of environmental pressures, pressures which are again beyond the remedies available to the social worker. In Bruce's case, for example, the mother, despite initially being seen as unable to provide the boy with consistent standards, had cooperated with the social worker to a degree which was thought to be sufficient for all practical purposes. The boy's continued offending, therefore, required an alternative explanation:

> Bruce obviously was a very established member of a fairly healthy delinquent sub-culture in the part of the town that he lived . . . It became increasingly clear that Bruce was taking much more of a leadership role than his tender years implied. The mothers of the sixteen years old with whom he associated would complain to me about how awful this little tearaway was, leading their charges into a life of crime. It became increasingly clear that there was an element of truth in that. But quite clearly the peer group being there and being in this sort of delinquent culture didn't help.

This type of explanation was by no means unique, as the following examples show:

> The main problems were delinquency. The family was emotionally intact and very supportive, parents very caring, both unemployed, but all the money seems to be spent on food, clothes, the place was well kept, clean and tidy. The boys were getting into mischief rather than any emotional breakdowns. One of the reasons why the children got into trouble was culture, there was a certain laxness about things.

*   *   *

I don't find this stealing a particular sign of disturbance, I mean that for somebody like Nicky brought up the way he has been brought up, it is actually quite natural for him, and his mother has brought him up to steal. He lives in an area where all the children steal. There it is just a quite natural law. It is not particularly a sign of disturbance whatsoever, as far as I am concerned.

Sometimes these two explanations, negative family influences and cultural pressures, are intertwined in accounts of delinquent behaviour. The social worker explained Tom's delinquency in this way:

> The mother colludes with the offences. I have never known her say 'That's wrong and you mustn't do it'. It is so much part of their culture on the estate on which they live, and it is in the family for them to steal. She doesn't see it as wrong really. She accepts the system is going to punish him but she doesn't really tell him off.

The third category involves those children whose acts defy explanation.

> It's a very difficult question because it came on so suddenly. We never heard anything of him until he was twelve. He seems to have had quite a normal childhood within the confines that he was fostered . . . But we never heard anything at all and then all of a sudden last summer he started to get into trouble and started acting up at school and things like this, and then the child guidance thing started which was a normal sort of progression and then suddenly he was in care and then suddenly he was offending the whole time and to try and work out why has just been very difficult. I really don't know.

*   *   *

> No idea. No idea honestly. It's quite a nice school. I mean there is no regimentation, he comes home officially every three weeks. I think he needs to be contained. I think that he may be asking us to contain him.

*   *   *

> I don't know. At first he maintained that it was bullying, that was well over a year ago. I liaised with the school over that and I don't think that there were any grounds for it. He went along for kicks with his friends. He is a bit of a coward so they may have said 'if you don't come we will do this and that' but I think that he was

willing to go. Since then he had done things on his own and he has admitted to it. I really don't know why, I mean the roll from Woolworth's. I don't think he is ever that hungry. When I have been round there, the mother has cooked quite decent meals for him. He wasn't at school at that time so he didn't have school dinners, he wasn't going to school. The tie and hankies from Tesco's that time, you can't really say that he needs them, that he was desperate for them.

Occasionally, social workers accepted the child's account of the offence and the surrounding circumstances. In these (rare) cases, 'need' was not made out and the care order was seen as inappropriate. Michael's case provides an example of this. The child was made the subject of a care order for his first offence while the social worker was on strike. The social worker accounted for the offence in the following way:

Michael would just go out at night when he came in from school. He said that he was very bored, didn't know what to do with himself, and they just wandered around the estate and got themselves into trouble. He said that very often they would be picked up by the police anyway, because they were known to the police, even when they hadn't done anything. They might just as well do something if they were going to get picked up anyway, so he put it down to boredom mainly. The care order was made primarily because, when he was living with father, his dad said that he was out of his control and there was no way that he would keep him at home under his present behaviour. So the care order was made because of dad's request. I think I would have been happier to have seen a supervision order really, where Michael could have stayed at home and we would have supervised him. I don't think there were the kind of emotional problems or anything like that in the family, although there is marital break-up. I haven't seen a lot of evidence of any kind of emotional disturbance in Michael. I think that if Michael is saying that he is getting into trouble because he is bored then supervision could certainly work round problems of giving him a few activities and talking to him, going out, doing things, and also working with the father helping him to cope with Michael's behaviour. Because at the moment we have kind of taken Michael out of the situation, made him extremely unhappy, and father doesn't feel any responsibility for the boy now, because we have taken over. And although he wants him back, as he says, he hasn't got a clue what to do with Michael now.

A similar point was made by Hardiker (1977, 1979) in her analysis of probation officers' ideologies when she contrasted probation officers' 'action accounts' of their clients' criminality (i.e., the offender's conduct is construed as determined in some way) with 'infraction accounts' (i.e., where the offence and circumstances of apprehension are seen as more important than the offender's needs). With respect to social workers working with children on care orders, however, the choice is rarely made between 'action' or 'infraction' accounts. The existence of the care order creates a pre-supposition that the child's behaviour lies within the 'action' frame of reference. But *within* that frame of reference there lies a range of options which affect not only the social worker's understanding of the case but his day-to-day practice. The ideological underpinning of 'what type of case is this' can be diagrammatically represented as follows:

Care *Cases 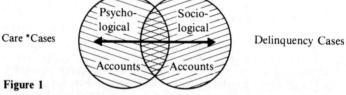 Delinquency Cases

Figure 1

*A more appropriate phrase, lexically, would be deprivation but we have chosen to use the language used by the social workers themselves to distinguish these categories of cases.

The more a case is accounted for in terms of psychological determinants and the less the child's delinquency is seen as significant, the more the case will be seen as a care case and, as a consequence, the whole family (natural or substitute) will be seen as the unit of need. Conversely, the more a case is typified in terms of action accounts and the more the child's delinquency is seen as significant, the more likely the case will be seen as a delinquency case and the child will be viewed as the unit of need.

In constructing this care-delinquency continuum we are not implying that cases are typified by social workers in an either/or fashion. The examples given on page 44 clearly illustrate the way in which social workers blur their explanatory accounts. What we are suggesting is that, at the polar extremes, cases are depicted as conceptually 'different' and 'distinct'.

Care cases are those in which the imposition of a care order after the commission of an offence is merely ancillary to personal or family problems which would have been sufficient for all practical purposes for the care order to have been made on other (non-criminal) grounds. The care order on the offence condition is, as it were, merely a legal convenience. The law was used as a resource to achieve competent professional practice (*see also* Grace and Wilkinson, 1978).

Lee, for example, was in care under Section 1 of the 1948 Children Act after his parents died. The boy was to have been made the subject of a Section 2 resolution (which vests parental rights in the local authority) when he committed an offence of taking and driving away a car which led to the making of a care order under the 1969 Act. When the social worker was asked about the boy's offences, she replied in the following way:

> Lee's care order is not because of the offences. Lee came into care because of his family circumstances, because he was an orphan and because he needed someone to look after him.

At the other end of the spectrum are the delinquency cases. Here the offence is the sole ground for the care order and the social worker's intervention is concentrated on that. Kevin, for example, had been found guilty of indecent assault and incest in the Crown Court. A probation officer had recommended a care order without prior consultation with the social services department. Because the social worker assigned to the case did not see the offence as symptomatic of underlying needs, he justified his response on the basis of the offence alone. Social workers locate the child between these two extremes and categories of 'cases' emerge.

The Meaning of Truancy

Truancy is a factor which aids social workers in their

interpretation of the case as 'care' or 'delinquency'. The majority of the children in our sample had poor school records and, in addition, many had had some prior contact with educational welfare services. (51 children [65% of the sample] had prior contact with either the educational welfare services or the child guidance service.) Emerson has written that truancy often provides evidence to those who judge delinquents that the child is moving towards 'serious delinquency'.

> Truancy not only suggests that the youth is a 'low achiever' and a behaviour problem at school, but also indicates that a great deal of his time is spent without control and supervision by adults (1969).

To a degree, this approach was adopted by the social workers we interviewed. In Gary's case, for example, the social worker commented as follows:

> Gary's basic problem is that by being out of school he has nothing to do so he gets into trouble, he gets into motorbike offences.

But, of itself, truancy was not sufficient evidence that the child was a 'real' or 'serious' delinquent. The initial location of the case by reference to the nature of the offence and the child's family relationships was far more influential in establishing 'what type of case is this?'. Truancy confirmed rather than shaped the initial interpretation of the case. In care cases, for example, truancy can be used as a further illustration of the 'real problem'.

> Well I think basically because of the legal thing really. He has got to go to school. We have to get worried about that. But there was also the thing that it seemed to be that the truancy was indicative of one part of other things as well. The whole lack of control that his mother had over him and the fact that, I mean the way I interpreted it, he was really in a very confused situation about both . . . He just couldn't cope with that and was just sort of shutting off from going to school.

Conversely, where 'infraction' accounts were used to explain the child's offence, truancy took on a different character.

His school is quite a large comprehensive school and it has got a headmaster who likes discipline and order and doesn't tolerate any deviance. He likes everybody to be dressed properly and to be neat and tidy, and he sends round little letters about how boys should tie their ties and things like that, and I think that he can't tolerate any difficult children, and we do find this, from this office, that it is a school who can't always tolerate a difficult child which perhaps another school would have tolerated him and helped him, but they weren't able to do so.

But truancy and school difficulties contained a further dimension for the social worker. School attendance, because it is compulsory, places on the social worker a legal demand which cannot be avoided. Within the wide discretion of the care order, it provides the one point at which action may be guided. It also places demands upon social workers which influence other elements of their practice. The law relating to school attendance, unlike the law relating to child care, is not used as a resource to enable the development of professional practice. Rather the demands for compulsory school attendance place limitations on the social worker in the way in which he can respond to pressing practical problems. The nature of school problems has to be interpreted against other features in the case but they also provide the social worker with a guide to what must be done. Hence in asking this question 'what type of case is this', social workers seek not only to establish what are the 'real problems' in the case but also to establish what they must do to meet those problems. Unless and until this is done social workers cannot begin to identify what the professional social work task is.

Routine Remedies

Implicit in our discussion of the question 'what type of case is this?' is the assumption that the answer provides social workers with a means of developing rational responses to an agenda of 'real problems'. The response chosen, we suggest, is accomplished by the social worker making competent judgements sufficient for all practical purposes. By this we mean that these judgements were made 'in light of "what everyone knows'' about the practical circumstances of work in general and on particular occasions' (Zimmerman, 1971).

By describing these decisions as 'routine remedies' we are not implying that, given the correct reading of the 'case', social workers act in a deterministic manner. We are suggesting that certain remedies are *usually* implied because they are seen as usually appropriate in the normal course of events for that type of case. Such remedies, therefore, not only provide for but also sustain the normal, everyday state of affairs. They are sufficient for all practical purposes for the production of a satisfactory outcome in meeting the 'real problems' in the 'case'. This does not mean that these routine remedies are necessarily 'successful' when adjudged by some criteria which outsiders (such as researchers) might apply (for example, whether or not the child commits further offences). But they are *appropriate* responses to the problems when viewed from the standpoint of the professional actor in the light of what 'everyone knows' about the 'real problems' in the case: his colleagues would do the same.

This important distinction clearly emerges from the following discussion with Patrick's social worker:

> The thing is that a boarding school will be well out of the borough, the opportunities for him to get into trouble won't be there. They will be home at weekends, and then possibly he will want to come home for weekends, and he would want to behave himself. Also personally I feel that he would get better education down there because, as I say, I feel he is an intelligent boy and in fact this has been proved at the assessment centre, that he can get down to school work, and I think that he would have a better chance of getting a better job, etc., better qualifications even, by going to boarding school.

Michael's social worker responded in a similar way when asked whether or not the children's home placement would solve the child's problems with his mother:

> Not really, no. The only thing I am hoping for is that Michael is strong enough to be able to cope with his mother better. Perhaps that is a bit unrealistic. He is quite a little kid and his mother is

quite big. He is quite meek really, he is not aggressive. Yes, I suppose I am feeling more pessimistic about rehabilitating him than I have been for a while really.

Though the decision making process cannot be described as determined, it is routinized. As Blaxter notes:

> Ideally in the medical model, as in the social work model, there is no categorization of the patient or his needs; each is individual. Yet in so complex a structure and with much of the work specialised and differentiated, labels are necessary and the organisation is likely to categorize the way in which best suit the task in hand (1976).

Gilbert Smith has also recently commented on this.

> In spite of the central position of 'discretion' in the imagery of professional social work, a growing body of evidence indicates that social workers are probably behaving in ways which are very much more highly routinized than is generally acknowledged, certainly by social workers themselves (1981).

Research has recurrently shown (Smith and Harris, 1972; Rees, 1978; Giller and Morris, 1978) that social workers seek rules, standards, categories and regular procedures so that they can, in Zimmerman's terms, 'bring off the day's work with respect to the constraints of timing, planning and scheduling represented by the described "actual task structure" ' (1971). The search for the routine remedy is not ideosyncratic or atypical (see Curnock and Hardiker, 1979).

What emerged from this research is that the closer the case was placed towards the care end of the continuum the more likely it was that the whole family would be seen as the unit of need and that the child would be kept within that setting. Conversely, the further the case was placed towards the delinquency end of the continuum the more likely it was that the child would be seen as the unit of need and that his removal from home would be sought. The social worker's choice of remedy was integrally linked to his depiction of the case. As one social worker put it:

I wouldn't think of sending Chris to a community home because I see C.H.E's for the delinquent, that's why I wouldn't think of that for him.

A distinct pattern of placements for care and delinquency cases was clearly discernible.

In care cases, intervention commonly took the form of returning the child home on trial and attempting family case-work or therapy. Where an immediate return home was not thought practicable, a children's home, hostel or reception centre placement tended to be used. Paul's social worker provides a clear account of this:

> The thing is that Paul, because of his small physical size, has been mixing with the wrong peer group. You know, he used to get very seriously bullied at school by kids who would perhaps be termed delinquent in the sense that they were kids who had committed offences, and the only way he has found acceptance and the only way he has managed to avoid bullying is in fact to join this group and there is no doubt that he is pushed into doing things, trying to be braver than all the others, his cheek, whatever. And that is another reason why I wouldn't want him to go into the community home system because he would then be just mixing with that very group. He is easily led.

Godfrey's social worker explained his choice of a local children's home in a similar way:

> In Godfrey's situation I think a large institution, given the fact that he is a shy and withdrawn boy, he is likely to be swamped by that type of set-up. Also I think it can re-inforce some sort of delinquent pattern. Yes, I doubt the value of it. It would mean being sent away, you know, given the fact that, although the father is quite ambivalent about his relationship with Godfrey, there is something there. Godfrey looks forward to actually going there. Now in terms of practicality, O.K., he can come home from community homes but I think that actually, you know, the children's home was, in fact, nearer.

The same point was made by Peter's social worker.

> I don't want him to feel that he is being punished because that isn't the major difficulty. The delinquent act isn't the major problem in

this family. And if he was to go to the community home he would be in with a peer group that has committed a lot of offences and it is likely that he will identify very strongly with them, he's already beginning to identify very strongly with them and he would most probably come out and be delinquent regardless of whether the problems at home are resolved or not. And the other part of that is that he is under achieving and I feel that he would be able to cope better if he had something that he felt was worthwhile. Education seems to be one area where he could do well. I have seen some of his work and he has got a good potential. So yes, at the moment, regardless of the education he should go away from home. But on top of that I, as a social worker, would be very unhappy if he was simply to go to a community home, simply because he had to be away from home.

In such cases, where the child could not be found a day school place due to previous truancy, alternative forms of education – such as intermediate treatment units or free schools – were arranged and where this was not possible, a boarding school placement (organised by the local education authority or a private body) was usually applied for. Boarding schools or schools for maladjusted children, although residential establishments with education on the premises, were seen as conceptually distinct from community homes with education on the premises. Paul's social worker elaborated on the distinction between boarding schools and community homes with education on the premises:

What I would prefer for Paul is a boarding school, whereby he can come home regularly for holidays and he wouldn't feel that he is actually in a place as punishment, he's not being deprived of his home full stop. A community home is much more like the old approved schools . . . I think that the community home is seen to have a kind of atmosphere of a thieves den. Basically children go to a community home because they committed offences. Boarding school is very different. Kids are not all there because they have committed offences. A lot of kids are there because they have family problems and the parents have asked for the children to have an education away from home. They can only cope with them at home during holidays, for instance, where they are a one parent family, where the mother may be very disabled. I prefer that Paul should have that kind of experience than one where it is lots of other kids who have committed offences.

Patrick's social worker expressed similar views:

> I don't think Patrick . . . usually boys and girls that go 'to community homes have done much more than Patrick's done. And I think that if he went to a boarding school . . . I mean loads of kids down there aren't necessarily on care orders, haven't got into trouble, and he would be mixing with people, ordinary people. Personally I think that if he went to community home I think he would get into more trouble. Also there is our own community home and boys get on very well there but I still think that in his particular case Patrick would get on better at an ordinary boarding school.

Apparent from these comments is the belief that a residential school outside of the community home system combined the essential prerequisites of a non-stigmatised removal from home and ample opportunities for home contact.

While removal from home was usually not the first option chosen by social workers in cases typified as care cases, this was not so in delinquency cases. Here the most commonly sought placement was for a community home with education on the premises. The social workers' taken-for-granted assumption about these placements was that they were schools for young offenders. The significance of the child's offence outweighed other considerations. Tim's social worker explained his choice of a C.H.E. in the following way:

> Well, I mean . . . I come back to the fact that he is in care, found guilty of what is a serious offence. If he is placed back at home he is back in exactly the same situation that gave rise to the original offence. The family do show a lot of interest in him. I don't think that he is going to be removed from home, full stop, but I think that a period away from home, settling him into a small group of about five boys of similar sort of age in a group home where he would also receive some form of basic training, or maybe take an outside job, where he can spend the time away from home with a group of his own peers which the file says he finds difficult to relate to.

Social workers acknowledged that they ought not to view C.H.E.s in this way since the intention behind the Children and Young Persons Act of 1969 was to establish an integrated system of resources for all children in need of compulsory measures of care.

> I know that a community home is supposed to consider kids with these sorts of needs but they do tend to get rather a lot of kids who have been in a lot of offences and I think that . . . I tend to use other things first, particularly if the kid is like Michael and has only had one offence, and I am not aware that he has been involved in other things. I know that the whole idea of the community home is that it should be much more open and that but . . . well the facts are that they haven't changed a lot and they do tend to take lads who have got lots of offences.

Nevertheless, the social workers attached considerable significance to the structure and discipline available in C.H.E.s. As Ray's social worker put it:

> In a C.H.E. he would know where he stood. At home it is very difficult, one minute mum's very critical and the next minute she is sticking up for them, one minute she is saying one thing and another minute she is saying another. Throughout the day Ray would know what he was doing. When he did wrong he would be punished immediately . . . and generally he would just know where he was and what he was at, rather than not really knowing.

Charma's social worker talked of the child's need for a C.H.E. placement in the following way:

> I primarily see the C.H.E. as providing some kind of security. There are so many cross currents of emotions at home over and above the normal cross currents in a normal family. There are so many mixed emotions in the home I think the C.H.E. is going to give her a bit of space. It is a straight forward regime. One gets the feeling that there is no messing, this is how it is, it is straight down the line, which worries me a little bit, but clearly from previous girls that have come back it obviously pays off, in the sense that they are not that straight. There is a lot more give and take than one at first felt. But I think that primarily it is security which is what Charma is needing.

While those social workers who had prior knowledge of the C.H.E. system added some refinements to their categorization (for example, C.H.E.s which were described as therapeutic

communities were seen to be suitable for the child who, while
delinquent, had some overt care problems, and those C.H.E.s
which were described as schools were seen as suitable for 'real
delinquents'), there were quite clear differences in the way in
which different forms of provision were viewed.

Nicky's social worker, for example, spoke of the distinction
between C.H.E.s with a 'therapeutic component' and those
without.

> The therapeutic component is that the place is run as a large family
> group. It is a very unusual, a very different place. They don't have
> shift working. Staff are basically available all the time. And I feel
> that this particular child, he would benefit enormously from being
> able to form relationships with staff members on a more family
> basis rather than on the system they run at community homes, the
> three shift system, etc. etc. That he might be able to overcome
> quite a lot of the difficulties he is having with his stepmother and
> father. At the moment if he can at least . . . have a good relation-
> ship with a neutral person . . . let's put it like that.

Finally, a C.H.E. placement was seen as providing a remedy
for educational problems: both the controlling aspect of
keeping children in school who would not otherwise attend and
providing a practically oriented teaching programme. Owen's
social worker summarised the compulsory nature of C.H.E.'s
educational provision in this way:

> Owen seems to be showing at the assessment centre that he has a
> fairly average educational ability, he doesn't seem to be retarded,
> and doesn't present too many problems at school there. He has
> said that he won't go to school if he returns home and we feel that
> a community home with education on the premises will be the best
> way to provide him with some form of education over these next
> twelve months when he would have to attend school anyway.

Implicit in accounts of routine remedies for delinquents is
the assumption that the social worker cannot achieve a satisfactory resolution to the problems in the case *himself*. The
significance of the child's offence and the assumed
intractability of the causes of it mean that the child must be
removed from what is seen to be a, prognostically, poor

setting. Yet, as the social workers' descriptions of C.H.E.s show, removal of the child from his home does not necessarily mean that the issues identified as 'real problems' will be resolved. In many ways, the negative assessment of the routine remedies for delinquents reinforces the social worker's negative assessment of this type of case.

We are suggesting in this chapter that the choice of a particular routine remedy is an integral extension of the abstract cognitive process of determining 'what type of case is this'. The bifurcation (at the extremes) of appropriate routine remedies mirrors the conceptual categorisation of routine cases. We can, therefore, represent the ideological underpinning of routine remedies diagrammatically in the same way that we presented explanatory accounts of cases.

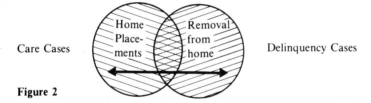

Care Cases · · · Delinquency Cases

Figure 2

As in the construction of the care-delinquency continuum we are not implying that routine remedies are typified in an absolute manner. At the extremes, however, the remedies chosen are conceptually 'different' and 'distinct'. In this respect also we must make a distinction between the routine remedy which is chosen and the routine remedy which is applied. Categorisations of cases and remedies must be understood within the constraints of social work practice. An examination of what Hardiker calls the 'exigencies of practice' (1977) is a necessary precursor for an understanding of decision making.

3

Ideologies and Practice

Remedies and Resources

Earlier we described how social workers construct a response to
the particular case before them. We suggested that the remedy
chosen followed naturally and logically from the social
worker's reading of the case and that social workers were very
aware of the appropriateness of different types of remedies.

Identifying a routine remedy, however, does not necessarily
mean that it will be applied. Pressing practical problems often
produce remedies which may disrupt the routine. Obvious
'problems' are when children abscond or commit offences
before any remedy has been tried. But 'problems' need not be
of such magnitude. In Michael's case, for example, the social
worker initially arranged to have the child assessed at the
regional assessment centre. After the care order was made,
however, the child returned home. The social worker explained
her actions as follows:

> The basic reasons why we agreed that Michael should go home was
> mainly that, due to the fact that the family were moving to
> Farnborough in January which hopefully would remove the
> environmental . . . it is not going to solve the problem completely.
> Also with Michael having temper tantrums all over the place, I felt
> that there was no way I could get enough support to get him into
> my car and down to the assessment centre. He said if he got into
> my car he was going to kick the whole thing to pieces, he was in
> that sort of state, and mum was almost backing him up in that,
> sort of saying 'Michael will do this and do that' and so on. So I, in
> fact, phoned my senior from the court and we discussed it over the
> phone and agreed that Michael should go home.

As a result, a contract was made with the child that he should stay out of trouble and attend school. If this arrangement broke down it was agreed that he would be removed to the assessment centre.

Similarly, in Donna's case, the social worker believed that the child was a quite violent adolescent and sought a secure assessment place. When this was not available on the day of the court hearing she placed Donna in bed and breakfast accommodation.

Yet what is 'a pressing practical problem' is not always an issue determined between the social workers and their clients. When social workers wish to do anything other than continue the casework relationship with their clients they are forced into interactions with other professionals in the child care system whom we can describe as the gate-keepers of resources. These groups carry with them their own taken-for-granted assumptions, biases and judgements, all of which may influence the final outcome of the case. We are not implying that these judgements are always in conflict with the individual social worker's. Indeed, there were few fundamental disagreements with social workers' reading of the case. Nevertheless pressing practical problems disrupted the routine remedy.

In John's case, for example, both the social worker and the local assessment centre agreed that the child, as a first offender, was in need of a local children's home placement. Difficulties arose, however, due to rapid staff turn-over in the borough's homes. After two months, the child was placed in a private home in Dorking. The social worker concerned explained the placement in this way:

> The recommendation was for a local children's home which I would also fully agree with. But, in fact, nothing came up in any of the local homes and eventually he went down for a visit to the Dorking home for another child who was being placed there and liked it a lot. Despite the recommendation that it should be a local children's home, because he liked it and they were prepared to have him.

The most common pressing practical problem, however, was

when social workers tried to place children in residential schools, outside of the community home system (boarding schools, schools for maladjusted children, etc.). Here, rules about the acceptable age ranges and the length of waiting lists often meant that social workers found that such options were unavailable.

Simon's social worker, for example, explained why he did not consider the child for a boarding school for maladjusted children:

> I think because of his age, because it was going to be a close thing whether we could get him in at all and as soon as Christmas went really it was going to be too late because they don't like to take children that are any older than . . . children they think they can do something with . . . so it is no use sending a thirteen or fourteen year old there. And also because he was offending so much and had been expelled from school. It was just most inappropriate to place him in a maladjusted boarding school.

Consequently, the child was placed in a C.H.E. Similarly, Marcus' social worker found that a long-standing application for a boarding school placement from the local education authority was refused soon after the care order was made simply because he was too old and and they were not fully aware of the family background. This child was also placed in a C.H.E. The social worker explained this in the following way, 'We're in the position of looking around for what is available, like, rather than what's right for Marcus.' Because such children were seen by the social workers concerned to need some residential provision, C.H.E.s were chosen often as the only available alternative.

These cases also seem to confirm social workers' complaints about the lack of resources for meeting the needs of children in care. But, like Rees, we have to ask:

> To what extent does that familiar plea 'lack of resources' reflect an identifiable lack of personnel and plant or a decision that some people cannot be helped in terms of how a social worker, immediate colleagues and others construe some ideal function of social work . . .? (1976 : 205).

It is necessary to investigate *as a problem in its own right* how social workers decide which children are appropriate (or inappropriate) for which resources and how, as a result, a short-fall in resources becomes acknowledged. Whether or not certain resources are seen as the desired routine remedy (and are, therefore, in short supply) may largely depend upon the social worker's reading of the case and his energy in seeking alternative remedies.

Discussions about the fostering of delinquent adolescents provide a useful forum for analysing the ways in which social workers' assumptions about suitability can short-circuit any serious considerations of a resource as a viable option, and, as a consequence, can place pressures on other facilities. In Michael's case, for example, the social worker replied to the question 'Why didn't you think fostering was suitable?' in the following way:

> Well because he is very fond of his family and his brothers and sisters are very special to him. I think that there might be too much conflict between his loyalties to his own family and his foster-family.

Similarly, in Veronica's case, the social worker, in discussing placement options for the girl, commented:

> Obviously I had a choice of looking for a fostering situation for her, but I felt that to drop her into a fostering situation was not going to be possible, and any way I couldn't guarantee to find foster parents. I didn't see it as being particularly appropriate given that here is a girl who is stealing persistently. She is, if you like, fairly out of control at present in terms of her behaviour and acceptance of societal norms and, therefore, I felt that it would be better for her to go into the local reception centre, and that was done in a way as I couldn't think of anything else to do.

But, as the comments of Paul's social worker illustrate, beliefs about the inappropriateness of this remedy are more important than its unavailability in practice.

> Because of the fact of his age, the placement was more than likely

C

to be a children's home rather than a foster placement. That's just
a kind of resources thing. Well, actually, it is just not a resource
thing, because I haven't thought about it too clearly because
resources wise it's . . . children's home is probably the only
reality, but, when I think about it, it would be a good idea for a
children's home rather than a foster placement which would
probably place too many demands on him in terms of his loyalty to
the individuals. In the children's home there are people you can
relate to whenever you want. But it is still not the same as a family
situation. He's got the family situation there to go back to without
living in it. I think that is the kind of idea that is coming out now.

The 'non-routine' nature of fostering placements for 'this
type of case' meant that serious consideration of this option is
often circumvented. Indeed, the existence of Special Fostering
Schemes confirms that; they are out of the ordinary (*see*, for
example, Hazel, 1978). We are not implying that fostering
necessarily works; we are merely highlighting that its present
exclusion from social workers' consideration when looking for
remedies must, *perforce*, limit the choices available to them
and sustain the belief that such a remedy is inappropriate.

It would be inaccurate to accuse social workers alone of
creating a situation in which certain remedies become routine
and others are not considered. Although the focus of this
research is social workers' decision making, much of the work
which they do is collaborative. Most significantly during the
early period of the care order, social workers make frequent
use of assessment facilities. This interface between social
workers and assessment centre staff is an important area for
investigation: answers to 'what type of case is this' and 'what
routine remedy is to be applied' emerge after negotiation between these two agencies. While the content of this process of
negotiation cannot be detailed here – our information on this
subject is too limited – we did investigate the assumptions
which underlie social workers' relationships with assessment
agencies. It is this relationship which forms the pragmatic
context within which decisions are made. In the words of one
social worker:

In any situation where you are involved with a kid who is in care, the decision making about his or her future revolves around a number of workers. Now those workers sit around and discuss what we think this child needs. Having decided what the child needs, that seems to me to be one point. You then have to look at what you can do with the child. There is often a short-fall between those two things about what the child needs and what is available. I think that is depressing and then the depressing thing on top of that is when you look at what is available, it is not very often available when you want it.

We previously suggested that a care order marks the stage at which 'problems' are given official recognition. Many social workers, however, felt that the child then required assessment. The purpose of this seemed to be to inform the social worker of the nature of these problems. When asked why they felt assessment was necessary, the following responses were given by social workers.

Well I felt the need for Paul to get out of the house, for more knowledge about what he was like as a kid. I mean it was very difficult to get that. As a social worker I see him . . . I saw him once a week or once a fortnight for half an hour or an hour, and it is very difficult obviously to know how he relates to other kids, what he is like as a kid. Even talking to school teachers you don't get that much impression of what he is like. Yes, so I thought it was important to get some kind of idea of what . . . of how he responded with other children and how he responded to other adults in an ordinary every day situation rather than to me as a social worker.

* * *

Basically a deeper understanding of what makes him tick.

* * *

I think basically that my assessment is based on a limited amount of contact with the kid in a fairly artificial situation. I might see him here on odd occasions but I wouldn't see him more than once a fortnight for about an hour and I think that in an assessment centre the kid is living in there and they are observing him over a fairly long period. I am not saying – my assessment probably to some degree compares with theirs but theirs is much more extensive, much more realistic. They can probably note things in

John's personality which I would never pick up by just seeing him once a fortnight, so my assessment makes a lot of assumptions about what is going on.

*   *   *

I think, you see, it is good to have another assessment on a child anyway. One can go into a family and one can be perhaps over-sympathetic either to the child or to the parents, not really see a true picture, so therefore a sort of detached assessment I think is very important.

Assessment was not always, however, thought to be necessary, at least in the first instance. This seemed so in two types of situation: where the social worker believed he knew what the problems were and where the child had previously been assessed.

The comments of Patricia's social worker illustrate the first point:

Well I felt that this was Patricia's first offence. It may or may not indicate some future criminal career. I think to place her in a secure establishment would be to confirm her with that delinquent label. if you like, and thought that it wasn't right at that time. And also I didn't accept that Patricia couldn't be helped in a non-secure setting, because I don't think it had been tried.

Richard's social worker provides an example of the second reason.

He spent a period at the local assessment centre about 18 months ago when he went down on a voluntary care order and was eventually recommended to be sent off on supervision. It is now two months since he came into care and I don't see very much point in sending him to the assessment centre for six weeks for assessment. If we decide that community school is on the cards then that may well have to happen.

But the social worker's view of the need for assessment could be effected by a radical change of circumstances. In Patricia's case, for example, the social worker's belief that the girl was pregnant altered events.

I wanted her placed at the regional assessment centre at one point for secure assessment because things had got to the point where she needed removal from the scene which she was getting into and we really needed to assess her which hadn't worked at the local assessment centre. That was the point when she ran away to Brixton and got herself pregnant.

The process of assessment is not, of course, a neutral fact-finding exercise (*see* e.g., Hoghughi, 1978; Tutt, 1977). The social worker concerned has already made a preliminary assessment of 'what type of case is this' before requesting further assessment. Underlying such requests are several taken-for-granted assumptions about what it would achieve.

First, residential assessment seemed to be used to confirm impressions rather than to discover new avenues for exploration. John's social worker illustrated this when asked to explain how his personal assessment of a child would differ from that of an assessment centre.

The cynical answer to that is that normally you get back what you said in your referral letter, what is given back to you in your feed back. So what I hope so far, from an assessment centre, a residential assessment centre, is first to find how a person responds to residential care, I think that is all you can hope for, because you can't find out that much more about the home situation than when the person was in the home situation, and normally you have got a good picture of the child from school, from youth workers here, you know. Very rarely, it has not been my experience to refer anybody I haven't had background information on. So because of that when I place someone in residential assessment I don't expect to get anymore than a response to residential care.

Or, as Steven's social worker put it:

I got an awful lot of information out of the assessment which in some ways was not new to me but confirmed my own feelings and ideas about him.

Linked to this was the belief that a residential assessment was a necessary precursor to a recommendation for residential treatment.

I have got a very terrible view of all assessments from meetings I have attended. I think in the main when you go to the regional assessment centre, or you take a child there, the end product is that the child will go to a community home, and they go through the motions of making it sound as though they are really concerned. But from the time that the boy goes in there you know at the end of the six weeks period that that will be the actual assessment.

Confirmation of this suggestion is found in the feelings of surprise which social workers expressed when a non-residential placement was recommended by the assessment centre.

So he was in a remand centre over the summer and then we got a place in the secure unit at the regional assessment centre so he went there and the assessment was started for community school. I was away on leave when the actual conference took place and the conference decided that Simon should go home and when I got back I was absolutely amazed that this decision had been made, I couldn't believe it. . . .

In Peter's case, the social worker had anticipated that the assessment recommendation would be for a C.H.E. placement. The case conference decided, however, that residential treatment was having an adverse psychological affect on the child and recommended that he be returned home. The social worker subsequently made the following comment:

I didn't feel that I could argue with the suggestion of mental breakdown if we insisted on staying there. I think it would have been very much worse for Peter to have stayed at the assessment centre and then him to come home and not go to school. C.H.E. would at least give him a chance.

This quotation illustrates a further assumption which social workers make about the assessment process: once the child has been given over to the assessment 'professionals', social workers feel that they have little control over the outcome of the events. In the majority of cases, this is not something which causes concern. Given that both the social worker and assessors 'read' the case in the same way, a mutually agreed decision as to the right remedy will emerge. Where there were disparate readings, however, social workers felt that they were in a subordinate position. As Elaine's social worker put it:

> In practice and in theory I should know more about the family than the other disciplines. But at the case conference if all the disciplines are decided on a point then I more or less have to go along with it, whether I like it or not.

The social worker's reading of the case was radically different from that of the assessment centre. He felt that people were exacerbating the problems because Elaine was West Indian (like himself).

> Because she is West Indian, lots of places want to escape responsibility. And more or less everybody is saying she is difficult, she is difficult. She is not really difficult, compared with other girls. Only one offence. Someone told me she is inclined to be very promiscuous and that is the worrying side. But I think that is labelling. Lots of white people think that West Indians are sexually aggressive. I think that is labelling Elaine and that is unfair. . . . But you can't rebel because it's tight. If you get the educational psychologist saying in reports, and he is a very powerful man, she is unstable because of x, y and z, and this is only a two hour session, the educational psychologist, you know, would have with this person and say unstable, and that report is based maybe on a few phrases, that a few people might say a certain thing, so that is labelling.

These feelings were particularly acute when the social worker in the case interpreted it in a different light from other professionals. In another case, the social worker described it in this way:

> At the case conference there was myself, the E.W.O. who I quite like, the senior and the senior educational officers, who were rather nice middle-class ladies. They were afraid that I being a young person should not be too afraid to take children away from home. The whole time they were pressing me to do as the conference says, remove the children from home. I was in a rather weak position because I couldn't dispute what was said about multi-preventive work having been tried.

John's social worker made the same point after the assessment conference recommended that John should be placed in a C.H.E.

> I think that it is soul-destroying when a boy has got some sort of potential but because of his behaviour he has got to be put into an environment like that, and there doesn't seem to be any facility for differentiating between a boy who can do better and the others, and he is just in a mess, you know . . .

The result is the same where social workers are sceptical about the assessment process.

> Remember long ago I was putting pressure on them to place her because they weren't doing much. The trouble is they have only around four kids down there now, in the local assessment centre, so all the staff attention is channelled on these kids. Every slight thing they do is blown up out of proportion. They are monitored now, which is a bad situation for the kids to be in. There was one idea I had once that was to place her in a local placement, with an ordinary family, but I don't think that was feasible because so many reports were saying that she needed to go into a community home, so I didn't pursue that one.

This 'powerlessness' was clearly illustrated at Paul's case conference. The usual procedure at the assessment centre concerned was for all of the professionals (social worker, assessment centre staff and the educational psychologist) to present their picture of the child and, in light of this, to outline his needs and those placements which would meet them. The decision concerning the appropriate placement would emerge, it was assumed, from this extended discussion of the child's position. At the beginning of this particular case conference, however, the boy's social worker stated that he had arranged for the child to be interviewed for a place at an independent boarding school. This produced great consternation among the conference participants and the social worker was rebuked by the chairman for preempting not only the work of the assessment centre, but also the point of the meeting. Paul's case was then discussed and, after 45 minutes, it was agreed that the 'proper' placement for Paul was the independent boarding school.

Despite the reservations which some social workers had about the suitability of certain types of remedies for certain cases, they seemed rarely willing to alter a placement once it was made. In John's case, for example, the placement at Dorking could have been ended and he could have been brought back to the local community home as originally recommended once the strike in the borough had ended. The social worker concerned, however, did not remove the child and explained her actions as follows:

> It would be desirable but you see . . . John has got himself nicely settled into the local school now, he is fond of the kids there now, and I would hesitate to move him again, and once a kid gets used to an environment unless I am very unhappy with it I'll leave them there. I mean it has got to be . . . things would have to be very wrong there.

Non-routine remedies were not merely something exceptional which the social worker had to tolerate; once applied, they vitally influenced any subsequent reading of the case. The remedy became routine. 'What type of case is this' could be reinterpreted to fit the remedy already applied. John's social worker, for example, had not recommended a care order for him.

> I think I would have asked for an opportunity to get the supervision order in process . . . you know I think I would have asked for a chance to see if one could work with the family or not on a supervision order and get that into operation before having gone for a care order. But for some reason, I can't quite evaluate my reason for this at the moment, it is somehow when children have been removed on a care order from a very bad poor home condition it somehow seems harder to permanently return them to that without having made some improvements for them to return to. I think had I worked with a supervision order and one would make an effort to improve the environment, home conditions, provisions for the childen, had that not worked one would have got to the stage eventually where we would have been forced to have a care order on the children by them just going back to court so many times probably. But now we have got the care order you have got that scene that you thought might come eventually, you have got it already, and they have been removed from you without

having worked on it. But until you have worked, you have got to be able to improve the home conditions to be able to return them home rather than working with the family to improve them. And I think that the other thing that has happened because I had a reasonably poor knowledge of the boys as individual people them having been in care and having had other people seeing the boys and having them twenty-four hours a day I have become much aware of their difficulties, how they function and at what level they have been functioning, whereas before I could only, in a way, think that this is what must be happening at home, and thinking that this is how they carried on and I never had any base to know that that was how they were functioning at.

In order to understand how social workers change their decisions over time, it is essential to address the dialectical nature of the concept of 'moral character'. Emerson explains this as follows:

> Actual case outcomes reflect the interplay between assessment of moral character and practical contingencies affecting what has to and what can be done about the case. An assessment of moral character may proceed independently of the negotiation and implementation of the disposition associated with that assessment. But it does set the conditions on which the (social worker) initially seeks to carry out these negotiations and implementation efforts. Again success or failure in implementing these decisions leads to a reassessment of moral character, as an initial version of moral character must be reconsidered in light of new alternatives. Thus, constant interplay between definitions of what the case is about (moral character) and negotiated outcome marks the progress of cases . . . (1969).

This interplay, we suggest, forms the foundation for an understanding of the dynamics of social work decision making in care order cases. In the following sections we concentrate on two areas which illustrate this: how casework ideologies are used by social workers and how cases come to change their categorisation over time.

Casework Ideology and Practice

Value judgements about people are at the hub of social workers' decisions (Rees, 1978).

So far we have suggested that the particular decisions reached by social workers depend upon their interpretation of the case before them. 'What type of case is this' and 'what routine remedy should be applied' are the two key questions which must be resolved before 'social work' can take place. The answer to these questions lies in social workers' judgements about the kind of children and parents they are involved with and their views about various resources and their suitability. In this section we explore how these judgements are used by practitioners to resolve the issues which they face in the light of pressing practical problems.

Care orders inevitably involve intervention with the lives of children and their families, but the nature of that intervention lies within the discretion of the social worker. A basic tenet of social work is the belief that children and families can and should be helped through the medium of interpersonal relationships: the ideology of casework underpins much of social workers' repertoire of responses. Yet while this ideology is recurrently 'discovered' in social work research (*see* e.g., Smith and Harris, 1972; Browne, 1978; Sainsbury, 1975) it remains ill-defined (*see* e.g., Timms, 1969) and is often ignored as a research 'resource' (Bittner, 1967). Rees (1978) has written that the mystical reverence given to the importance of 'the casework relationship' can be maintained only to the extent that 'it does not depend on empirical evidence of what social workers' actually do.' This section concentrates on social workers' accounts of casework and suggests that 'doing' casework can be very different from theory.

Creating 'the casework relationship' was usually described to us as the first task for the social worker. Given that the child's delinquency was frequently seen as a symptom of 'wider problems' – primarily within the family – it was natural that these were seen initially as the intended focus of social work.

> I think mum . . . can be quite a manipulative lady. She will try and twist things round so that things seem perfect. There is quite a lot of work to do with her, getting her to understand even basic child-care principles, such as basically bringing up kids properly, or

what a social worker would see as middle-class type ways, I suppose. It is difficult to explain. I sort of want to try and help, to put it in social work jargon, to come to terms with her own inadequacies, stretching her capabilities . . . I think the major problems are her inconsistent attitude towards the kids, they get their own way one minute and sort of sat on the next.

Other social workers expressed similar opinions.

Because the problem is situated in the family I have still got to work with the whole family initially, and a lot of work would be needed with mum just by the very fact that she will be living alone. I know that she is going to find it very very difficult to live alone. I mean one small instance is that she is scared to stay in the house on her own, sleeping, because she is used to having one of the children sleeping with her. So over the weeks that they have been remanded in care, they have been on Section 1, she has had to come to terms with that. And there are a lot of other things that she will need to come to terms with. And also I would like to help her as a person, sort of build up her own self-image, because she has got so much going for her, but she really has a very poor opinion of herself, and to work on that. And also to work on her sort of attitude towards the boys and towards child care. I think that if she thought more of herself as a person, then she would be less demanding of the children and could give them more as a mother.

*   *   *

I can see a role in trying to get mother functioning as a more adequate part of the family, as a more important role in the family, because I do feel she is able to do far more in the family. But father has got this sort of thing that he has this need to envelop all the worries himself, take on all the responsibilities and because of that he hasn't coped. Now, things have got too much for him and he has been trying to help them function far better between themselves. I see that as a role, but in fact one needs to work at getting mother far more involved and for her to see what is going on in her family.

Establishing 'a casework relationship', however, seemed more than a professional practice; it carried with it a judgement concerning professional worth. Cases in which the development of a casework relationship was possible were seen as hopeful; where this was not possible, the social worker's role changed.

Research has already pointed to difficulties in establishing a casework relationship with working class clients (*see*, for example, Mayer and Timms, 1970; Sainsbury, 1975; Rees, 1978). What emerged from this research was that, when these difficulties arose, the clients tended to be reclassified. In Gary's case, for example, the social worker described how the boy's continual absconding from the regional assessment centre and the consequent pressure from the local councillors and the police to have him apprehended forced her to reassess her role.

> I mean up until that point I had always been very concerned about Gary's emotional state and individual needs, the usual sort of things I would be concerned about. I think by this time I was beginning to withdraw from that sort of . . . it was almost as if I was dropping my social work role and just sort of being a local authority employee.

The social worker in Bruce's case, faced with Bruce persistently refusing to return to his community home, responded in a similar way:

> I mean I couldn't go back into the, if you like, the counselling role, the getting deep into the situation and looking at past events and everything, because I was dealing with the practical aspects of getting him back there, and, ya, I felt well I couldn't do that, not in the short space of time I was working with him or with the family, I had to do it a lot more subtly and a lot slower and I think I have tried to get that over, learning by our mistakes sort of thing. Whenever Bruce has gone back I have gone over, round to the mother and talked about it, but mainly I say 'Bruce has got to stay and you have got to get him back when he is not going back', things like that.

But even where there were no such pressing practical problems and where it seemed possible that a casework relationship might develop, there was no guarantee that it would. Failure by the clients to perceive their problems in the social worker's terms would produce equally unsatisfactory results. In Donna's case, for example, the social worker clearly expressed frustration at the mother's inability to talk about the 'real problems'.

> I think that the focus tends to be with the mother and that is not necessarily my intention, she is a very demanding lady. There are times when I have tried to reduce the amount of contact on the work that I am doing with her and try and make it so that I see her once a fortnight because . . . well you get drawn into the family, you get drawn into her personal feelings and she is always saying that she is cracking up and she can't stand it any more, and she goes on about housing, she externalises everything to the housing, and to a large extent that tends to over-shadow what you can do with the kids individually, that is why I try to get them in here one at a time. I think that the focus has tended to be on the family situation and I am going to try and contain it. But they are under a great deal of pressure. It is an awful place to live; once there were five kids sleeping in one room, and Paul was the only boy and he was getting pushed out, and the adolescent girls didn't want a young boy sleeping in with them, so it was necessary initially to overcome this housing problem, try and work on the relationship within the family as a whole, It has become increasingly evident, to me, when you start a case, you plan it, it could go in this direction, but the case makes its own demand, so increasingly you tend to get pulled in by the mother and it becomes increasingly difficult to work for good relationships within the family because she is only interested in housing and that reflects on the kids. They are only interested in housing; they see that as the be-all-and-end all of their problems.

The clients' reluctance to participate in the casework relationship produced similar results:

> I think really we will not get far with the mother . . . not unless you have got a lot more time than I have got . . . it would take so long to build up any kind of relationship with her which she would be actually able to talk about. I think she just, well partly because she is very decent when you go and then she is so untrusting of anybody in authority, and I don't blame her, it makes working with her very difficult.

It was not uncommon for both of these difficulties to be present in the one case.

> I have never been able to talk to mum, not even since the care order

has been made. I tried to make an appointment to see her when I came back off strike, I got no reply when I knocked at the door, but father came to the office when I made an office interview for him to come along. Dad's attitude to it all is that he is very concerned about the offences. He used to get quite upset that the boys were doing it but could never see that it was probably his boys at fault. It was always these other boys that were naughty boys who lead his into trouble. It was always the fault of other boys, never his boys.

Parents' attempts to disassociate themselves from their children's 'problems' were also frequently cited as reasons for failure to establish casework relationships.

Mother has got a very funny idea of what she thinks social workers should be doing. She was extremely manipulative at first, and even now. 'Money, I want money, I want a new settee, I want this, I want that, you can get it'. And if I didn't then it was shocking. Very, very difficult to try and work with her. And earlier it was 'you're Tony's social worker, you're not mine'. But gradually she has accepted me and will talk about other things that happen that don't concern Tony. There were problems with the father when she had to justify my going round, it was because the court had said I had to go round to see Tony and then, of course, if I mentioned the other children, one of the others, say Paul, that there was a problem with his schooling, mother would say 'you don't come here to talk about my children. They are my concern. You come here come here to see Tony'. It makes it very difficult to divorce Tony from the rest of the family. Their problems obviously affect him and he causes some of theirs.

Such a strategy made it possible to retain a casework ideology while casework practice was postponed.

If you have got a particular focus, say you are doing a bit of marital crisis, say you are working intensively, maybe for instance on a three-day contract on sorting out their relationship, that kind of thing, you have got something to bite on and that can sometimes come up with adolescents. But I think it is much more difficult because of the difficulties that most adolescents have in terms of being able to verbalise their feelings and so on. It is the lack of that something to bite on. You lack something you need as a basis to get down to a working relationship. I am thinking in terms, not necessarily of kids who are in care but who are supervision orders and the reputation of having kids on supervision orders has around this . . . it is that kind of thing. It is impossible to work with them so what can you do. They will come in and sit and you will say 'well how are you getting on and so on and so on' and sometimes it is all right and sometimes something can develop over a period, if you don't make too many expectations of them, and you are quite clear about why you are there. I think that if you draw the boundaries very clearly, exactly what is going on, then, even though within the session they might not be able to articulate or use the session very well, after a while they do actually start to trust you, but it is a very slow process.*

What seems to happen in such situations is that social workers interpret the case as one which is not amenable to casework techniques and which, therefore, requires other resources. John's social worker described this process in the following way:

Now we have one problem, one great problem, which we are trying to overcome with John: his complete denial that he needs any extra help and there is anything in a way abnormal with him. He has made this strong thing already that he is not going to go to any training centre. He has refused to go back to his local school which he was at prior to the care order because he said that is for nutters, which makes it very difficult when you have got a child who is totally, in a way, refusing to acknowledge his own limitations.

The description of the case as 'hopeless' was facilitated by the emergence of additional problems. Not only was John seen as 'abnormal', but his denial of this became a problem in its own right.

We are not implying that social workers act in some calculated and conscious way in ascribing the case with such an aura of scepticism. Expectations of 'good' or 'bad' cases are not merely shaped by social workers' personal philosophies. The organizational structure within which they work does much to sustain such definitions. Moreover, social workers themselves are very aware of these organizational pressures. As one social worker put it:

---

*For a similar response from other social workers see Giller and Morris, 1978.

I think a lot of social workers have a very unclear conception of what their role is, not just for kids, but generally speaking. I run into an awful lot of difficulties because they think that they expect that they should be taking a much more personal relationship than is actually feasible, or in some senses, desirable, in the bureaucratic structure that you are working under.

So, even where social workers acknowledged that some of the problems in the case were not entirely of the client's making, they often felt constrained by their position within the agency to initiate further action. The social worker in Elaine's case described how one such situation came about:

The care order hasn't achieved anything. I mean if the mother was a fairly good mother she could have gone to court and said 'look you haven't done anything for that girl. You have just taken her away and more or less locked her up in the local assessment centre, isolated her from the family.' It might have been a better situation to give intense social worker help with the family and Elaine in the family rather than paying out large sums of money to keep her at the local assessment centre. She is always absconding, I mean it is madness. She is back now, but she is always absconding. There is nothing being done. The establishment and all the reports on Elaine say she is a difficult girl and she shouldn't be at home. So for me to do that, I would be sticking my neck out and I am not prepared to do it on this one at this point . . . I am fairly new to this scene . . . only been working for nine months . . . powers would be brought against me to say 'Look you are new to the game, other people have a lot of experience. You haven't got experience about social service.' It would be foolish for me to stick my neck out and say 'Now we haven't done anything for Elaine, she should remain at home.'

A similar response underlay those cases which were interpreted as delinquency cases. Here cultural, social and economic forces were frequently cited as the causes of the delinquency to explain why casework techniques were not used by the social worker.

Given that Oliver had in a lot of ways already a fairly deprived sort of childhood or, up to now, that there are certain areas of him which perhaps haven't developed as strongly as they might have been with a kid with a very strong family and that sort of thing. I don't know that it is actually possible to go in a flash and have a care order and in eighteen months make up for a lot that has not been there for fifteen years, really.

*   *   *

Well because I think probably that is all one can do. I can't go out and change the neighbourhood or stop him getting involved with his peers, and one wouldn't want to anyway . . . Because he has got to do it on his own. You know we are not going to be around forever and well, there are certainly enormous areas of these kids' lives that one dreads to think what they get up to, that you would never really be able to be involved with.

Another social worker described how he coped with these apparently 'hopeless' cases.

If you are doing a job like this, I mean, alright this is a bit of a cock-up, but if you actually end up doing a job like this you can't do anything about those other things, or you wouldn't want to, or you couldn't cope with it, or you would be a community worker or a social policy person, or that is what I think. You do actually choose the bit that you can work on. But I suppose that I do think that families make or break people in the sort of world that we live in, and the sort of status that the unit has and what it can provide. I think that it can make or break people.

Social workers seemed pessimistic about their ability to effect change in delinquency cases. One social worker, for example, contrasted a case in our sample with another in his caseload:

I have got a kid who came into care before your sample started as a kind of comparison because that one I do view very much as a totally structural kind of thing. West Indian kid, in this area, the family is fine; there are things in the family that you could say were causing him to be delinquent, but I don't particularly think so and I view that as being caught in the kind of delinquent culture living in Notting Hill in 1978. It means that I am much more pessimistic about the situation for a start. And that is the other reason why social workers do tend to concentrate on the relationship things. If there is anything in the relationship that they can naturally grab a hold of because it is the only bit that you can actually feel that you might be able to do something about. Except, to be cynical about it, that this is actually not going to do

any good really because the rest of the whole structural thing
is . . .

Another social worker described the air of hopelessness in this
way:

> Well you picked my worst case. It is the one I always feel most
> desperate about. Because mother is very manipulative, because
> father is violent, when you go in for an interview it is a very
> difficult situation and Tony catches a lot of it, especially mother's
> manipulation. When I went to see him in the assessment centre,
> 'Have you got any money for me? You got some fags?' and I said
> 'no' and he snatched my bag away. He didn't open it, I mean, he
> was just messing about. When I look what he has been through
> and when I look at the background and the culture and the
> acceptance of the delinquency within the family and now his
> brother's started. He wasn't at all worried in court and that was his
> first appearance. He just wasn't at all bothered about it, and when
> I tried to talk to him about the offence . . . 'I don't. I don't' . . .
> He just wasn't going to talk to me at all. I feel that there is often a
> block because of the mother and the way she has of getting
> through. There just isn't the fear of the court, the police with them
> and they just don't have any conscience about it. This is what other
> welfare services have said. The Superintendent at the children's
> home feels that Tony would do anything for money, even homo-
> sexuality. There was some question a while back. He just hasn't
> got any scruples at all. He just wouldn't be at all bothered, and, in
> a way, I can see that.

In those cases in which the child became the focus of
attention – either because of the family's refusal to become the
'client' or because the child's delinquency was seen as the real
problem in the case – social workers often felt constrained to
remove the child from his home. In these situations, however,
few social workers claimed to be acting as 'professionals'.
They felt that they had to assume a bureaucratic or managerial
stance and acted as coordinators between the various parties
involved.

> I think it is a role of sort of coordinating because if it breaks down
> we have got to keep an eye on things. If it breaks down you will
> have to find another placement, things like that. Also I'm
> somebody else he can ring up and talk to about all sorts of things

and liaise with the C.H.E. about things that may be going wrong. It will also involve being aware of the family and home situation here, to feed that into the C.H.E. at case conferences and things. So we have got a full sort of outlook on the whole situation. It depends on how things change or don't change.

*   *   *

In cases where children are in community schools, work with the mother as such is not detailed, it's only in connection with the placement to the school, communication and when it comes to discharge, preparing the boy's return home. So I don't casework the mothers usually. My involvement with the boy is the reviews. With boys in community schools I tend to visit once per month to see how things are going and have a chat with the boy to see if he has any problems, you know, any difficulties, what his relationship with mother is, how week-ends are going. So these are the main lines of attack with him because there are usually social workers there at the school who are doing a lot of casework.

This bureaucratic or managerial stance did not involve the social worker in actively participating in the case. For all practical purposes and in the normal run of events, he remained detached from it. In such situations, many social workers spoke of not being fully in control.

My experience of juvenile justice is that it can be a mechanised procedure. It is like an escalator. When you are on it it is very difficult to get off it. You might be fortunate to jump over the middle section and get onto the one going down, but you can't deviate very easily at all. So you kind of, you feel very much that you're a kind of passive actor in the situation and can't personally gate-keep on the escalator, that is the kind of metaphor.

Their acceptance of this role was often compounded by the practical impossibility of participating meaningfully in the child's life once he was removed from home.

Well I shall probably visit, see him, see his headmaster at a maladjusted school, see how he is getting on and watch the holidays, see how they go, and when he goes home for weekends watch how weekends go, just keep an eye on Richard and his home, Richard and his school. He is probably going to be quite a long way away, rather difficult to do anything intensive as he is going to be quite a long way away. It will probably be sort of term visits, and seeing him in the holidays.

Once the child was removed to a residential placement, the case no longer retained the immediacy of a pressing practical problem in the social worker's caseload. As such problems continued to present themselves daily, the 'settled' case was placed low in the order of priorities.

In Veronica's case, for example, the child was removed to a local assessment centre to determine what the 'real problems' were. On one occasion, during this placement, the social worker made the following remark:

Now last week, and this week in terms of my own job, I have been extremely busy and in terms of lack of priorities, or deciding, you know, which am I going to respond to first Veronica had not been top of the list. Therefore, I have not been on the phone to the assessment centre or physically been round there to see what is doing, what's happening. So as far as I know she has been at the assessment centre since that date and attending the educational unit.

But in addition to the fact that maintaining continuing contact with children was 'inconvenient', once the child was placed residentially there was also a widely held belief that it was 'inappropriate'. As one social worker commented:

Now the child's in the children's home, I'm in the back seat in terms of organising things and making the decisions. I don't think that it is my role to try and establish very much more than a working relationship with him. I think that it is the role of the residential staff to get through to him as a person and develop that, rather than me. Apart from that, I think it is easier for them than me having a session every couple of weeks or whatever, I think that is work that the residential staff should be doing and I think that is the way they see it as well.

Many social workers felt, however, that the adoption of this bureaucratic or managerial role generated negative feelings amongst their clients. Paul's social worker, for example, in response to the question 'How does the boy see you now' made the following comment:

I think Paul sees me as a rather distant figure, because I came in at a very late stage, who is most probably meting out punishment to him, because he has gone back to the assessment centre. He is going to be taken to some kind of residential establishment and, though he has voiced the wish to do so, the amount of choice is limited, and, therefore, he obviously sees me as a controlling figure.

The more social workers adopted this bureaucratic, managerial stance the more they were removed from the possibility of establishing a first-hand relationship with their clients. As long as the routine remedy continued to work, this distance posed no particular problem for the competent management of the case. When unexpected events occurred and when the routine remedy broke down, however, social workers found themselves in a difficult position. Inevitably, they were then asked by those who had day-to-day contact with the client to resume responsibility for the case. That is, social workers were asked to move from their bureaucratic or managerial to a social work role. But this earlier detachment of the social worker from his client meant that the social worker was not in a good position to answer 'What type of case is this?'. Consequently, the social worker was forced to rely upon the impressions of significant others in the case (e.g., residential workers and assessment centre staff) to provide him with information. To the extent that the comments of others were negative – and in the case of placement 'problems' they were very likely to be negative – the case was likely to be reinterpreted as a delinquency rather than as a care case.

Casework ideology provided no sure guideline to practical action; more significant were social workers' interpretations of people, attitudes, events and roles. As Rees notes:

> Running through social workers ideologies (are) assumptions about worthy and unworthy tasks and, at least by implication deserving and undeserving clients (1978).

Consequently, the social worker's reading of the 'moral character' of the case was essential to an understanding of how decisions were made.

The Dynamics of Decision-Making

Earlier in this chapter we discussed the interplay between responses to the questions 'what type of case is this' and 'what routine remedy is to be applied'. We will now examine what is meant by social work decision making. Decision making, we suggest, demands that the social worker makes an assessment of the 'moral character' of his clients (both children and their families) in the light of the pressing practical problems in the case. These assessments, however, are not fixed; they are made when a case is allocated or reallocated, when placements are successful or breakdown, when children reoffend or stay out of trouble, when parents cooperate or refuse to cooperate and so on. In fact, reassessments can occur at any stage. Hence cases change, improve or become worse not necessarily on the occurence of some objective state of affairs (such as reoffending), but instead whenever the social worker *perceives* some event which questions the application of the routine remedy. This is not to say that a pressing practical problem may not be associated with events such as reoffending, absconding or a placement breakdown. But these must be interpreted against the routine, taken-for-granted background of the case. It is only when these events challenge the social worker's reading of the case that a fundamental or real change occurs. Then social workers feel that they are making a decision as opposed to administering, bureaucratically, the mechanics of routine cases.

The majority of the social workers we interviewed applied routine remedies. It is not surprising, therefore, that few of our cases were fundamentally reassessed during the six month follow-up period. After all, routine remedies would not be routine unless they usually worked: the problematic became the mundane. Social workers 'managed' the majority of their cases and other matters could take precedence. Kevin's social worker illustrated this process in the following comments:

> I don't think the case has changed much. I don't think the basic situation has changed much. I think I have got a more realistic attitude towards it now. Whenever you start, you start with the

ideas of what you hope to achieve and how you are going to do it, and very quickly the realities set in. I think I told you when I first started that I would aim to see Kevin weekly to start with. I have just been checking out how often I do see him and, in fact, it was weekly for the first two weeks and then with sickness, a course, and a holiday knocking out the next ten weeks, that very quickly went by the board. And what I have fallen back on is, in fact, that I see Kevin quite often casually because I am around the area where he has been hanging out. I then tended to see him once a fortnight, and I have been more authoritarian recently than I would have thought of being at the start because Kevin opts out and goes on without any sort of direction. So I have tried giving him a bit of direction to see what that would . . . so in a sense I have changed my tack. I am not working with the family as much as I was because that situation has settled down a lot. When I started the house was filthy, everyone was in a panic about the kids. Dad was speaking about putting them in care. Dorothy (Kevin's sister) seemed a very lost little girl. I think now Dad has worked out a reasonable compromise between working and looking after the kids. Dorothy seems much more confident and settled in what she is doing. The house is much cleaner. I suppose it still leaves a lot to be desired, but by the family's standards it is much cleaner. Generally our agencies involved are not as panicky as they were to start with.

We are not implying that social workers neglect their clients, but rather that social workers, like all of us, must get through their workday and that, to achieve this, assumptions are made about what is and is not problematic. As Walter notes in discussing social work with delinquents in a residential setting:

> The working day is simplified through developing 'recipes' of action for dealing with the standard kinds of situation which emerge with this type of (case). 'Individual treatment' does not happen most of the time; indeed, were it so, staff would very quickly resign for it would entail the abandonment of the recipes which simplify everyday life and enable us to act (1978).

In order then to examine how decisions are made, we must look at the atypical and the idiosyncratic. It is only when the taken-for-granted assumptions about everyday life break down that they become apparent. One such category of case is where the care order is no longer seen to be the appropriate remedy.

Usually in these cases the child was placed at home and subsequently stayed out of 'trouble'. In Peter's case, for example, the social worker initially had a low estimation of the ability of the parents to change their approach to child rearing. The following comment was made during our first interview:

> I think that one has got to realise that with a lot of these families whatever you try and do you won't change them. Why should you really try and change them. You might feel that you would like to, but if you do this, that or the other, or if I had them this way or that way, everything would be so much different but that is their way of life and they are not ever going to change whatever you do. And in a way, why should you, but obviously you have got to be concerned about the kids.

The social worker's original plan was to remove Peter to a community home. Soon after the care order was made, however, she decided to return the child to his family and explained her reasons as follows:

> Possibly because in a way I feel I get on well with mum. And regarding father, although he was going to opt out of the situation, I seriously think that this is what he meant to do, but after the interviews in the office and in the home, one got to know him a hell of a lot more and I possibly thought at the time that if Peter went home I would work with the parents more.

After six months the social worker was very pleased with the progress made in the case. She described the boy's achievements in this way:

> Well, I mean, he has stopped mixing with lots of kids who when he was offending he was mixing with. He seems to have left them behind and he has joined lots of clubs on his own without our pushing him at all, and I think he himself realises that if he does anything else he possibly might be sent away from home and so he is really trying hard. At the moment though I say he is trying hard, it is just coming naturally to him now that he is fitting into the family.

Moreover, even if the child were to reoffend, the home placement was felt by the social worker to be the most appropriate.

The way I feel at the moment talking to you, I hope he doesn't reoffend obviously, but the way I see it at the moment, if he did reoffend, I hope we could still retain him in the home, because it is working well and I think it is for Peter's benefit.

The level of improvement was such that the social worker encouraged the parents to apply for a revocation of the order.

This case illustrates a further point, a point which may in fact explain 'progress': the power which the care order gave to the social worker to remove the child from his home was seen as an important motivating force. According to the social worker:

Peter realised that the local authority could place him at various places. I think this had helped him to try harder to live within the family and I think it helped me to work with mum and dad more.

Martin's case was similar. The social worker returned him to his parents after the care order was imposed for a first offence. Although the offence was seen by the social worker as relatively serious (burglary of a shop leading to £300 worth of damage), he placed Martin at home 'to see what the real problems were.' In the social enquiry report prepared for the juvenile court, the social worker had presented the ambiguous nature of the child's offence in the following way:

In his eleven years, Martin has received extremely inconsistent handling from adults, a long separation from his mother and father who have been violent towards him. We feel strongly that Martin's offence has been committed as a result of family tensions and does not necessarily reflect delinquent leanings. It is difficult however, to ignore the seriousness of the charges, the extent of the damage done to the shop window and the amount of money involved in the theft. It does not appear that this has been spontaneous but rather planned behaviour. We must, therefore, consider whether these offences are not simply reflecting family difficulties but a definite attempt on Martin's part to get himself removed from the family.

Over the following six months, however, the social worker was increasingly satisfied with the progress of the case. The child remained out of trouble and the parents fully cooperated with the social worker when she visited the home. On our last interview with the social worker, she described the case as 'a very nice case; everybody's talking, everybody's co-operating. It's one of the better ones really.' The earlier suspicion about the parents' moral character – that they abused their children – had disappeared.

> It is not what my category of child abuse is about, I see the father as a big hulky guy who hits them . . . it's not what I define as a battering parent. And I don't think they are different now. I think because they are scared and because we said quite clearly that we don't approve of them . . . it is all a matter of degree and relativity and how much they are hitting and how much they are punishing. I think if that supervision goes on and that good relationship remains they are amenable to self-restraint.

In addition, the boy's efforts at staying out of trouble served to minimise the significance of the offence and to make the case no longer a pressing practical problem.

> From what I know of Martin he is not a bad kid at all. Before the offence he had not done anything wrong, it was an isolated incident. I mean I only met him at that point so I didn't really know him. He hadn't done anything before that, he hasn't done anything since, and, according to his teachers, he has always been quite good. They were very surprised as to what has happened to them all. I think that he was particularly upset at that time over his father . . . the thing is that they were beaten at that time. . . . he could have been upset, but I am . . . but I really don't think that he is really delinquent . . . He has been channelled into being a sea cadet just now. It has taken all his energy . . . he is quite happy living there and he is not getting involved in any sort of delinquent activities. I do feel that the mother too needs to talk about the boys to someone and she does talk quite a lot to me, and I think that will continue.

A further example of 'progress' is Michael. His care order (for a first offence) was made on the recommendation of the social worker; but she said she was a reluctant participant to the decision:

> I suggested a care order. That was on the basis of a consensus of opinion at the case conference, but I haven't really been happy

since Michael has been remanded in care. The worker who was mainly involved before that was the E.W.O. I wasn't seeing the family at all. So it was very much my recommendation based on the consensus of opinion.

The child was to be placed in an assessment centre once the order was made but due to an outburst at the court the child was returned home to his mother. A contract was then made with the child that he should stay out of trouble and attend school regularly. Subsequently the mother appealed against the care order and, after 20 weeks, a supervision order was imposed in its place. The social worker agreed with this change.

It is my opinion that over the three or four months that Michael has been at home the situation could be worked on a supervision order as easily as it was being worked on a care order.

But, in addition, the social worker could not ignore the fact that the child had stayed out of trouble since the care order was made, even though that improvement may have been coerced by the circumstances.

I think that Michael has been very aware of his appeal coming up, and I think he has made a very conscious effort to hold himself up. When I go round he is always on his best behaviour, his hair combed and looking smart and this sort of thing, which on the whole is to impress the social worker who is there.

Nor could she ignore the cooperation which she had received from the mother. All of this confirmed her initial feelings:

If I had known the family six months I would have backed away from the care order. . .

A second category of case was those which gained the social worker's support because the non-routine remedy which was applied actually worked. In Bruce's case, for example, the social worker had decided to remove the child from a residential school and to return him home. The social worker explained his actions as follows:

It didn't appear that they were offering a particularly considerable input into his education, and he was saying that he didn't feel particularly stimulated during the day. I don't know, that may have been just an excuse on his part. I think more important is the factor that his relationship with home did seem to be improving, getting better. Mother was saying that she was finding him much easier to talk with, he wasn't staying out, he was back by reasonable hours, he wasn't just ambling out and telling her to get stuffed if she asked him where he was going, that sort of thing, and he just seemed to be a much politer lad, much more amenable, and for that, he confessed that he was also a bit bossy with some of the siblings, quite demanding of their attention as well. But there were indicators that things were improving.

Similarly, the initial anxiety about Della abated as a result of subsequent events. Della had been brought into care after assaulting another girl. She and her family had been known to the social services department for some time and there was considerable anxiety concerning her case. The social worker revealed this anxiety when she first described her plans for the girl.

I have dealt with violent girls before but there is a rawness to Della's violence which in my own experience is unique, right, and the department themselves, our principle management adviser, reckons she is one of the most disturbed girls we have got, one of the most disturbed youngsters they have had for a long time. I think an ideal placement may well be a secure unit. Literally as a moratorium. That is the only opportunity you get to hold a child, at least not to let them deteriorate too far before it's too late, as it is in some cases. She would be there for about a year.

On the day the care order was made, however, there was no available place for the girl in secure accommodation. Faced with an impending strike, the social worker hastily arranged for the girl to stay in bed and breakfast accommodation. After four months, the social worker returned to work and, much to her surprise, found that Della had maintained the placement. As a result, the application for the secure unit was dropped and the social worker began to look for a hostel place. As the social worker put it: 'She's the sort of young lady that I'll let be while she's doing O.K.'

But not all changes in the way in which cases were assessed were positive. Cases were moved towards the delinquency end of the continuum when unexpected events were interpreted negatively. In Paul's case, for example, the social worker initially depicted the problems as care matters. As the child could not be returned home immediately due to the mother's perceived inability to cope, he had been placed in a local children's home with the condition that he attend school regularly. This arrangement lasted for over four months until Paul's truancy came to the notice of the children's home. The head of the children's home then called the social worker in to discuss the problem and an arrangement was made whereby the children's home would more closely monitor Paul's attendance at school. A second meeting was arranged a week later to assess the situation. Here it was agreed that Paul should remain in the children's home. At this stage, the social worker also canvassed the possibility of finding an alternative day school for the boy but this was seen as a contingency plan for the autumn term (some 3 months off). The day before the third meeting with the children's home the social worker received a telephone call from the head of the children's home saying that they were going to remove the child. The social worker described the events as follows:

> The head of the children's home phoned me yesterday to say that Paul still wasn't going to school, and the fact that he is around and not going to school and getting away with it is having a disruptive influence on the rest of the house to the point when half of them were beginning not to go to school. The head of the children's home has got a very big thing about all the kids at his home going to school. Quite rightly he pointed out that he had laid down a condition in the very beginning and that it had been agreed then that the assessment centre would take him back if the children's home placement broke down. I'm not very pleased at all about the way that it has been going. It seems that the children's home just kind of decided at some stage to give up on him, and have been pushing to get him out ever since. I can moan a bit about the fact that they seem to have given up on trying, but I can't do anything about that.

The child was subsequently returned to the local assessment

centre. As the situation evolved, however, the social worker gradually moved from his previous insistence that the child should not leave the community. The pressing practical problems became such that the case had to be reassessed and residential school then emerged as the inevitable and logical placement.

> It has certainly closed the options quite a lot but, in fact, even before, well after the last meeting at the children's home, I was thinking about the points they were raising there in terms of 'is it possible to work in terms of the family and would it not be better to have him actually quite a distance away and just work with him.' I have been thinking about that and I am beginning to come round to the idea that it might be better for him to be more clearly away from home for a while. But I am not sure how much I am coming round to that simply because it is the only realistic option that is open to me now, and it is difficult to tell how far it could have been different now if the children's home had handled it differently. It is more or less impossible to work with mother in terms of her insight in the family although it might be possible but not in the way I have been working. It might still be possible in terms of finding a support so that she can reach an adequate level of looking after herself. But certainly in terms of the family dynamics it is more or less impossible to work with her and I agree with that. And the fact that Paul has not been able to . . . rather than use the children's home has gone back home all the time and has not really been able to get any distance to look at it, to look at what the home situation is about, that is what is pushing my thinking in that direction.

The techniques originally used to answer 'what type of case is this' were subsequently used to deal with new pressing practical problems. But events were not always as slow to change as they were in Paul's case. Reassessment could be quite rapid. Steven's case illustrates this point.

Steven was a fourteen year old boy who had come to the attention of the local authority only a few months before the care order was made. His parents had notified the social services department that their child was running away from home and that they could not cope. It was during one of these escapades that the child committed his (first) offences. Steven was placed in a local children's home and a care order was made to discover what the 'real problems' were. Soon after the order was made, however, the social worker decided that Steven's behaviour was a direct product of his parents' marital disharmony. Consequently it was agreed that the child would remain in the children's home for a while and would attend local school and that a series of family therapy sessions (involving the child and his family) would be undertaken over a three months period. The social worker explained this as follows:

> I think we felt that family work should be tried because this was a family with potential and a boy that wasn't a typical criminal and seemingly offending for less than the usual reasons. If that didn't work and the family weren't prepared to hold him then we were thinking in terms of a hostel or one of our own resources, if they are available, and working with the family at the same time.

The family therapy sessions began and the child was returned home with the parents' agreement. Within a few weeks, however, the child ran away again and committed a further offence. He was then remanded on an unruly certificate prior to the court appearance. The social worker at this point made it clear that the character of the case had radically changed. Now, and in total contrast with the first interview, the case was depicted as beyond the remedy of the social worker:

> The first three sessions of family work went fairly well. Everyone was pleased with the progress, the family were making concessions, they were negotiating with time keeping. Mum was concerned that he was using the place like a hotel, and we looked at the things where he could show more consideration, and they could perhaps show more ability. His sister was pretty uncooperative which was just a way to screw him up because I think she wanted it to fail. Then there was a three week gap and Steven's family started taking in all the rope they were giving him. It didn't break-down though. What is interesting is that the family allowed him to break all the rules that they had laid down in family sessions. They didn't say 'No you can't, that is not in the rules we laid down' and he started going out at night, having more money than he should have, not staying indoors for five minutes, and they let that go on for three weeks, at the end of which he offended. I suppose you could deduce that there was a need for Steven to fail. The thing

about the sessions – that was five or six weeks – was that he was being set controls, and he enjoyed it. The marriage had been avoided at all costs, they refused to discuss it, and even when they came on the 30th, when Steven had disappeared, they refused to talk about their relationship. So they are not open, so I think partly there is a need . . . for Steven to fail for some obscure reason . . . there is a need for Steven to have controls and if they are not there he will offend.

In addition, the social worker clearly began to regard Steven as a 'real delinquent' in need of a different remedy. In this respect, the subcultural association in the boy's delinqueny was highlighted:

I suppose you could add up that he is in with a guy like Colin (the co-accused) who has been a criminal since he was ten, he has been a delinquent since he was ten. And it is a very seductive experience for Steven, he enjoys this, the energy, the status of it. What seems to have happened since is that family scapegoating still exists, but that it has been reinforced by his peer group and the excitement, if you like, of reoffending and we are caught now with trying to treat both.

Consequently, the problematic nature of interpreting the boy's behaviour became pronounced:

I don't know, Steven has said on more than one occasion that he wants to be punished, and maybe there is something in this boy that does, and so I guess that it is possible that, it is just possible, that he may stop offending.

The social worker recommended, and Steven received, a detention centre order when he later appeared in court. On his release from detention centre, the social worker considered placing Steven in the regional assessment centre with a view to a community home placement. He explained this in the following way:

Removing Steven to alternative accommodation deals with the family problem as well as the other problem. You take him out of the family. In a sense that deals with the problems of the family in that it allows him to develop apart from his family, out of the

D

pressures that they may place on him. It doesn't deal with 'the' family problem and in a sense that has become less relevant because our prime concern is more with Steven and so we are dealing with his individual pathology in relation to his family and his peer group by removing him. I don't think one ignores the cause. I think one decides . . . yes I think one is treating the boy as a result of failure to treat the family . . . and that is about all there is to say. We seem to have no alternative.

With respect to future parental involvement, the social worker continued:

We saw the parents after that, while Steven was still in detention. They were basically giving the same message. They were saying 'Well he has learnt his lesson now.' They would let him come home, but they didn't really want a social worker involved with them. They felt that any problems that they might have had were long in the past; it was totally irrelevant now. They are not open to us getting involved, they are resisting any attempts.

At our final interview, the social worker summed up the case:

Six months ago one would not have regarded Steven as a delinquent, but in a very short time he seems to have established that reputation.

This rapid shift of perspective was not unique. Barry, for example, began his care order in a residential boarding school run by the local education authority. After absconding and committing an offence of TDA, he was removed from the school. He returned home while awaiting his court appearance and was subsequently given a detention centre order. (No recommendation was made by the social worker.) The social worker depicted this case as one which had rapidly deteriorated over the four months leading to the detention centre order. While the boy was in detention centre, the social worker had the boy assessed by written reports for the C.H.E. place. The child returned home briefly on leaving detention and (shortly after our six months follow-up) was admitted to a C.H.E. At our final interview the social worker said:

Maybe I shouldn't have placed him in a boarding school, I would have gone straight for a community school placement had it been available. I think that a boy like him, without a father figure, would need a firmer type of control and structured type of environment which one would find in a community type of school.

Similarly, Malcolm (again a first offender) was placed first at home, then in a children's home, next an observation and assessment centre, and, finally, in a C.H.E. all within just over the six months. During this time, the social worker's view of the case changed dramatically. Initially he had resisted the care order and felt that a supervision order was adequate. In our final interview, however, he said:

> I believe basically that this lad is so knowledgeable about drugs and delinquency and that sort of thing, it is a latent thing, he's waiting for the right opportunity. I think that probably, when he's discharged from care in the next 2 or 3 years he will go the way of his father.*

But before any fundamental reorientation can take place, social workers must evaluate the entirety of the case. Events by themselves may have no dramatic impact if other elements in the case sustain the social worker's original interpretation. In Godfrey's case, for example, the child stole a watch from a store while home for the weekend from his children's home placement. The social worker, however, accorded this act no particular significance.

> You have to realise that this child is going to need a lot of long-term love and care and obviously there aren't going to be miracles.

This interpretation of the event could only be sustained against a background knowledge that since the child had been in the children's home he had 'started to come out', that previously he had been shy and withdrawn and that the head of the home was keen to keep the child with her.

What we are suggesting in this chapter is that the social worker's reading of 'what type of case is this' is conditional. Definitions of the case and the remedy to be applied only hold

---

*The boy's father was serving a prison sentence for drug offences.

'until further notice' (Schutz, 1962). They may be held for the entire duration of the order. On the other hand, there may be dramatic relocations of the case and the remedies to be applied over a fairly short period of time. The fact that cases can move so rapidly through the care/delinquency continuum underlines the importance of the assessment of 'moral character' in understanding social workers' decision making.

4

Ideologies and Rhetoric

I would advise you to set aside your therapeutic ambitions and try
to understand what is happening. When you have done that, the
therapeutics will take care of itself.

Sigmund Freud

Throughout this research project we have attempted to suspend
the taken-for-granted assumption that social workers'
decisions concerning children who offend are rational,
professional judgements based on some predetermined
objective criteria. Rather we have asked a fundamental
question: What does it mean to make a social work decision for
those who make them every day? Notions of 'rationality',
'decision making' and 'social work', therefore, have become
problems in their own right.

To illustrate our point, let us take the recent definition of the
social work task provided by the British Association of Social
Workers:

Social work is the purposeful and ethical application of personal
skills in interpersonal relationships directed towards enhancing
the personal and social functioning of an individual, family, group
or neighbourhood, which necessarily involves using evidence
obtained from practice to help create a social environment
conducive to the well-being of all (BASW, 1977).

This definition is perhaps the best recent example of the
obfuscation which surrounds analyses of the helping
professions. Indeed, some have argued that the function of
such rhetoric is to support social work's claim for professional
status and for a special sphere of operation in individuals'

affairs which it could not support otherwise (*see* Cypher, 1975; Pritchard and Taylor, 1978). Social work theory provides little in the way of guidelines for social work practice or for analysing what that practice is. Yet before an accurate knowledge base of what social work *is* can be provided, what social workers *do* must be a central concern (Curnock and Hardiker, 1979). Throughout this study we have concentrated on one element of practice: decision making. We have argued that social workers do not have clearly developed theoretical principles which can be applied and assessed. Rather, like Rees, we suggest that social workers make sense of their job

> through the development of practice-oriented ideologies . . . sets of ideas about categories of cases and means of dealing with them. These incorporated work routines, typified people's problems and staff's roles. They enabled the staff to manage what most regarded as an occupational hazard of having large caseloads and too little time and other resources to deal with them (1978).

In coming to this conclusion, we are not suggesting that social workers' practice ideologies are atheoretical. Clearly social workers *are* aware of concepts such as 'good enough' caring (CCETSW, 1978), of the Eriksonian categorisation of the stages of child development (1965), of casework theory (Reid and Epstein, 1971), of the labelling process (Becker, 1968) and the like. But as Browne has commented:

> Perhaps it is because the concepts . . . of most practice theories are too general and therefore not readily translated for application that social workers make scant reference to theory (1978).

Consequently, social workers use practice ideologies to assimilate issues, events, people and behaviour. In this way, pressing (and non-pressing) practical problems may be identified and coped with. Social work theory forms an element within that assimilation but, of itself, it is insufficient to dictate action.

Underlying these practice ideologies are judgements – judgements about people, their problems and the ease with which the social worker believes he can, and wishes to, deal with them. By posing the question 'what type of case is this' social workers categorise the problems and work priorities involved in each new referral. In this way, cases become identifiable as 'easy' or 'difficult', 'short-term' or 'long-term', 'hopeful' or 'hopeless'. When social workers can create an agenda of problems, mutually acknowledged with their clients, which gives them a meaningful role to play, the case will be accorded a high priority in the social worker's time and effort. Conversely, where the problems cannot be defined, are not acknowledged by the client or provide no meaningful role for the social worker, cases will be given a low priority. The meaning of criminal offences must be interpreted against this backdrop of the social worker's assumptions of what is and is not worthwhile social work.

By seeking an 'explanation' for the problems before them, social workers attempt to minimise the significance of offences. If they did otherwise, there would be little for them to do. The construction of a genealogy of causation, therefore, is essential so that actions may be 're-interpreted to accord with the social worker's paradigm of problem definition' (Hardiker and Webb, 1979). Other signs of trouble such as truancy and glue-sniffing are used to place the criminal behaviour in some context and, of course, thereby, it loses its uniqueness. Moreover, the willingness of the client, especially in this regard the parents, to be coopted into the social worker's reading of the case is vital. By locating the 'real problems' of the case within the family setting and by coopting the clients to work within it, the social worker is able to contribute directly to the remedy. Such cases provide 'good work'. Cases capable of being interpreted in this way not only provide social workers with the opportunity of exercising techniques which they favour but also of acting in a way which is highly regarded by their colleagues.

This must be contrasted with those cases which are not amenable to such interpretations. Here the child's delinquency remains a distinct focus of concern and the social worker is unable to locate the problems squarely within the framework of family dynamics. Moreover, the latent rationality of the child's behaviour makes the social worker's *personal* influence on his client more problematic. The unwillingness of these clients to be coopted by the social worker underpins the assumption that they will not 'change'. Hence the social worker believes that the scarce resource of his time will be wasted. A lack of optimism in the social workers concerned is the hallmark of these cases. The perceived intractability of the problem means that clients tend to be separately identified: parents as one category and the child as the other. In such cases, removal of the child from the family becomes the inevitable response to enable the child to develop insight. Awareness (which the worker can provide) is replaced with the need for consistency, structure and discipline (which the social worker cannot provide). As one social worker put it after placing a child in C.H.E.:

> I would have preferred it if he had stayed nearer his mother, not necessarily at home, but near. I suppose it's partly because it's so hopeless, or I think it is. The point is it isn't actually. I think that it's practically hopeless. The more hopeless you think it is the more you shoot kids out as far as possible which is what I have done . . .

Having evaluated the case, the social worker then begins to construct a response which reflects the judgements he had made. Cases which are amenable to change, in which the clients are cooperative, in which 'good work' can be done remain an active part of the social worker's caseload. Cases which are thought to have these qualities tend to be placed in children's homes or boarding schools until 'something happens' which indicates more clearly what type of case it is. Finally, cases which have few positive features, both in terms of the intractability of the problems and the social worker's role in dealing with them tend to lead to placements in C.H.E.s. These routine remedies, as we have called them, could, of course, be disrupted by the exegencies of everyday practice (such as lack of places, problems with age limits, etc.) but as a general representation of the ideological terrain of the social worker's world they are accurate. They are what usually works for this type of case.

But the question 'what type of case is this?' is not detached from the issue 'what routine remedy is to be applied?'. Social workers' judgements about the type of case not only influence the remedy chosen but their judgements of the people and problems in the case. Remedies which use the social worker in only an administrative way (such as arranging leaves or attending reviews) are not seen as providing the social worker with a real social work role. The case, therefore, becomes seen as not as worthwhile or as rewarding as other areas of work.

We are not implying that social workers' judgements are fixed once the case has been read. Assessments of the 'moral character' of the case hold only until further notice. Each contact with a client, each event, each review produces new information about the case which the social worker must assimilate into his background knowledge of 'what type of case this is.' It is this process of assimilation which social workers illustrate when referring to 'getting to know a case' or 'becoming aware of the problems.' But in some instances, the information defies assimilation; the social worker is led to question his taken-for-granted assumptions about the case. Consequently, the case becomes another 'type' and the original remedy no longer retains its routine quality. It is these assessments and reassessments of the case, either positive or negative, which underpin social workers' decision making.

Suggesting that social workers' judgements only hold until further notice does not mean that a completely fresh assessment of the case is made each time an unexpected event occurs. The truly 'investigative stance' (Zimmerman, 1974) is only possible when the social worker asks 'what type of case is this' in the first instance. The need to identify the 'real problems' then makes it imperative that a full investigation is made. Thereafter, further assessments are made in the light of what is already known about the case. But the generation and control of information which affects the reading of the case is not always in the hands of the social worker. Clearly, for example, in placing a child in a residential establishment, the social worker must rely on the statements of others as to the child's abilities, progress or difficulties. Structurally, the social worker is not in a position to make a full investigation of events or to evaluate them on his own behalf. Moreover, the recognition that those who provide residential services are competent professionals denies the legitimacy of any attempt by social workers to do so. Even when the social worker has reservations about the services provided, he may feel unable to voice them.

In one of our cases, for example, two brothers were placed in the same C.H.E. some considerable distance from their home. Initially the boys expressed great unhappiness with the place-ment. After a month, the social worker received a letter from a residential worker at the C.H.E. saying that he believed the placement to be totally unsuitable for the boys. The letter told of how the boys continued to be unhappy and how, in the opinion of the residential worker, the continuation of the placement would actually harm the boys. The social worker, alarmed by this unofficial message, notified the headmaster of the C.H.E. and insisted on a meeting to discuss the issue. At the meeting, the headmaster glossed over the issue by saying that the residential worker concerned was a very unstable character who was about to leave. The boys' unhappiness was explained as the 'usual' response from children who have been removed from home. While driving back to London, the social worker expressed considerable frustration to one of us with the way in which the matter had been dealt and voiced serious doubts about both the ability of the C.H.E. and the manner in which she had been treated. She accepted, however, that she could not investigate the issue any further and had to accept the headmaster's account or remove the boys from the school. The latter course was ruled out because the social worker felt that she would receive no help from her assessment centre colleagues in finding a 'better' place.

The purpose of reporting this incident is not to say the social worker was 'right' to be sceptical about the C.H.E. or that the headmaster was 'wrong' in his handling of the case. The point is that the 'outsider', the social worker, had only limited powers to investigate the issues involved. The social worker ultimately *must* rely upon the evaluations of professional others that a placement is or is not working or that children are 'good' or 'bad'. All of this integrally affects the assessment of the 'moral character' of the case.

But even when social workers retain control of the case and can, therefore, acquire and evaluate information at first hand, a radical reassessment of the case may not be avoided. The examples of reassessment in Paul's and Steven's cases illustrate how easily this may occur. We suggest, however, that pressing practical problems stand a greater chance of not being viewed negatively when the social worker makes his *own* evaluation than when he must rely on the evaluations of fellow professionals. This is because both positive and negative information is continually being generated and assimilated by the social worker at first hand and placed in the context of what he already knows. Implicit in this is the suggestion that when fellow professionals bring issues to the notices of the social worker they are more likely to be of a negative than a positive kind. Put simply, a child who is disruptive and aggressive in a placement is likely to come to the social worker's attention whereas a child who achieves all a placement can offer within a short period of time is not.

In Brian's case, for example, the social worker attended a review at the boy's C.H.E. During the review the social worker voiced, on the child's behalf, his dissatisfaction with the education programme which was available. The boy said he had already covered the subjects offered at the C.H.E. while at day school and that the range of educational opportunities in the C.H.E. was too limited. The headmaster responded that the education programme was currently being restructured and that, in time, Brian would benefit. The headmaster ended his comments, however, with the statement that, if the social worker felt that the C.H.E. had nothing more to offer the boy, he should remove him.

Similarly, the social worker in Timothy's case spoke of how the boy had completely changed in the three months he had been in the C.H.E. The boy was now regularly attending and enjoying the education there and his family relationships had improved dramatically. When the social worker mentioned these matters to the senior staff in the C.H.E., he was told that the boy had 'a long way to go' and that premature removal of the boy was out of the question.

We have seen that, for the majority of our social workers, working with delinquents was mundane, routine and unrewarding. There was little in the way of pay-off either in terms of changing clients, establishing worthwhile relationships, or being seen by colleagues to be doing a 'good job'. Social workers only retained and actively participated in those cases which they evaluated positively and which were seen to be amenable to their efforts. To seek actively to establish a casework relationship with a delinquency case was not only seen as a non-routine remedy, but as a waste of resources given the overall demands of caseloads and other pressing practical problems. There was a positive incentive to remove such children from their homes, to engage other professional helpers and to concentrate on what was sufficient for all practical purposes: managing the case in a bureaucratic way. Residential assessment provided social workers not only with an ever-open door for discovering what the 'real problems' in a case were but also with a way of diverting 'hopeless' cases. Since residential assessment is a good predictor of a recommendation for a residential placement (S.S.R.I.U., 1977; Cawson, 1979), this meant that these children were continually being diverted from direct contact with social workers. Furthermore, social workers' perceived powerlessness in relation to assessment professionals and their lack of detailed knowledge concerning different kinds of placements meant that there was little active participation in the subsequent decision making process.

This, of course, is only part of the paradox of the 1969 Children and Young Persons Act: the increases in the number of children placed in institutions. Whereas Charles Morris (1978) has located the source of this paradox in economic considerations, our research suggests that both structural and ideological issues have produced this result. We agree with Morris, however, that social workers must be given positive incentives to retain control of these cases for this situation to change.

We are not suggesting that social work in the community

would be more effective at preventing recidivism. The evidence which exists suggests that this is not so (Brody, 1976): social work in the community seems to be as effective or ineffective as residential work. What we are suggesting is that, currently, decisions which are said to be based on the needs of an individual child are, in fact, routinized. Moreover, the results of that routinization are such that decisions bear little relationship to any particular quality of the case or any 'rationality' which can be ascertained by 'objective' criteria.

This is where the fundamental difficulty in understanding the nature of social workers' decision making (and, concomitantly, in any attempt to change it) lies. Decisions about children who offend are decisions about 'moral character': they are essentially moral choices. Hence, reforms which merely alter the structural arrangements within which social workers make decisions are not, of themselves, likely to alter the nature of these moral choices. For example, the recent proposals to introduce a residential care order would not resolve it. Instead of leading to a thorough-going appraisal of the 'proper' use of care orders, a residential care order would provide social workers with a routine remedy which would legitimate the belief that working with delinquents is not worthwhile.

It seems that social workers already avoid work with delinquents: it is only where delinquents can be viewed as really care cases that the social workers retain them. Indeed, so embedded are the values contained within social workers' judgements that their very elucidation is problematic. Few social workers in our sample, for example, talked in terms of making a 'decision'. Responses to the pressing practical problems in the case are talked of in terms of being inevitable remedies which emerge from the case. Consequently any change in the case does not imply that the social worker's initial decision was wrong or bad. For all practical purposes, the ascertainment of moral character and the application of the appropriate remedy typically achieves what the social worker wants. It provides social workers with an organised way – which is usually successful – of exercising their power. The individual social worker is concerned that he has exercised 'competent use' of his power and that his decisions were reasonable in light of that use (Zimmerman, 1971).

So far we have concentrated on the world of the social worker and the way in which he develops practice ideologies of delinquency and control. We must now place these issues in a wider ideological context. As we have argued elsewhere (Morris and Giller, 1978), the history of juvenile justice policy in this country is an attempt to amalgamate the various categories of children with whom the juvenile justice system has to deal. The assumption underlying the 1969 Children and Young Persons Act is that offenders, like other children in trouble, are not responsible for the circumstances which bring them before the court. Consequently, the focus of attention has moved, in theory, from the *conduct* of the juvenile to his *status*. Delinquency is viewed as only one of many of the expressions of 'secondary poverty' (Crosland, 1964) which was revealed with the expansion of the Welfare State. In other words, the 1969 Children and Young Persons Act marks the apotheosis of the liberal theory of crime in the sphere of juvenile justice policy. Hall *et al* (1978) have outlined the elements of this theory.

> The criminal is seen as backward, or bored, or confused, or ignorant, or poor, or under socialised: 'Forgive them, for they know not what they do.' The individual agent is a weak vessel, with the power of forces larger than himself. Only the mechanisms of socialisation and good fortune keep the majority of us on the straight and narrow. When these 'socialising' mechanisms break down, all of us are vulnerable to the revival of anti-social instincts and impulses. Crime is at root a 'social problem'. It arises, not from some fundamental premise of the whole moral universe, and not from some major structural fault of the social or moral system, but from particular failures, particular lapses in a structure which remains, in large measure, sound. Social problems require solutions. If the social or psychological processes can be remedied and improved, the possibility of such behaviour recurring can be minimised (1978).

Set against this view is what Hall *et al* call the conservative explanation of crime. Here the stereotype of the delinquent is not the social casualty but the conscious perpetrator of social disruption. Although juvenile delinquency is viewed primarily as a personal problem, it is assumed to arise from personal iniquity rather than social inequality. The appropriate response to juvenile crime, therefore, is not solely the provision of social help but the correction of the offender by discipline and punishment. The basis of this conception is individual freedom in return for responsibility for that freedom.

In practice, the 1969 Act has perpetuated both these conceptions of the juvenile offender. The full machinery of court room adjudication and criminal penalties are retained for those seen as responsible for their actions while social welfare services are available for those seen as the 'non-responsible' products of their social circumstances. But, as this research suggests, the operation of these ideologies in practice is not an all-or-nothing picture of responsibility or non-responsibility. Social workers employ a variety of explanations of criminal behaviour in the particular circumstances they are confronted with. As Hardiker notes:

> Whether the offender is seen as determined or freely acting does not follow from the personal ideology of the (social worker) *per se*, something neatly parcelled before the client is even seen (1979).

In his reading of the case, the social worker may employ case-work or treatment concepts or, equally, he may decide that the child has exercised free will in his actions. The liberal and conservative ideologies of crime are distinct but not mutually exclusive. Social workers may hold both and thus the specific form of intervention chosen may be legitimated by either perspective. Furthermore each perspective contains areas of overlap within which the various practitioners in the juvenile justice system may come together to produce working solutions to their pressing practical problems. At the extremes, of course, these ideologies generate different criteria of judgement in deciding whether or not a particular decision is competent. Juvenile court magistrates, for example, frequently expect care orders to provide a remedy for juvenile delinquency and social workers' decisions to relate in some way to the nature and circumstances of the child's offence. Where this does not occur, the social worker may be seen by the magistrate as responsible for the subsequent delinquency of the child. On the other hand, sometimes there is apparent agreement. Social workers may justify a detention centre recommendation on an ideology of individual need; magistrates, however, may see the same solution as necessary on retributive or deterrent grounds. This means that consensus as to the appropriate intervention in a particular case can conceal real conflict in ideological positions. In this way, ideological differences which surround the present debates on juvenile justice policy become masked by the rhetoric which enables the day-to-day operation of the system to be passed off. To adapt the words of Bittner, practice-oriented ideologies of crime 'emerge as a generalised formula to which all sorts of problems can be brought for solution' (1974).

It is only where practical solutions are contested that ideological conflict becomes pronounced. As May and Smith have written in discussing the ideological differences between the practitioners of the Scottish children's hearing system:

> Clearly such rhetoric is functional to the extent that it enables groups and individuals with conflicting interests and claims on the system to come together in an increasing and precarious alliance in order to accomplish certain specific tasks. Such collaboration is essential if the system is to survive as a 'people processing' organisation (1979).

By examining members' accounts of their 'professional ideologies' and 'operational philosophies', the real nature of this conflict becomes clear. An analysis of social workers' decision making in relation to children in care provides a foundation for this discourse.

There is increasing pressure to change the juvenile justice system in this country. Research should precede any such change. Our present findings, for example, suggest that social workers readily intervene in the lives of children and their families. Over half our sample received their care order on their first or second court appearance, the majority of our sample were removed from their homes on the making of the care order; few children were returned home once placed residentially and those children placed at home did not reoffend more frequently than those in residential institutions. Although our sample is small these findings are confirmed by Cawson's (1979) research and suggest that much of the moral panic over the practice of care orders is misplaced. Moreover, current proposals for the introduction of secure or residential care orders would do little to alter the position. Reforms must meet their objectives or they will be counterproductive.

Appendix

i. SAMPLE

Boys	*Girls*
68 (86%)	11 (14%)

RACE

Black	30 — 38%	*White*	49 — 62%
Boys	20	Boys	48
Girls	10	Girls	1

ii. OFFENCES FOR WHICH THE SAMPLE CAME INTO CARE*

	No. of Offences	*No. of Children*	*%*	*Cawson's Sample %*
Violence (inc. robbery)	8	6	6	9
Burglary	47	23	22	38
Theft	76	37	35	66
TDA/Road Traffic	28	27	20	12
Criminal Damage	12	12	11	9
Sexual Offences	3	3	3	1
Other	4	3	3	13

*Based on the 79 children coming into care during the sample period.

iii. PREVIOUS DISPOSITION*

	Boys	Girls	Total %
No previous dispositions	30	5	45
Fines/Discharges	29	6	45
Attendance Centre	14	—	18
Detention Centre	1	—	1
Supervision Orders	20	1	27
Care Orders	7	2	12

+N = 78.

*Categories of dispositions are not mutually exclusive
+Excludes one case for which we were unable to collect information.

iv. NUMBER OF PREVIOUS COURT APPEARANCES PRIOR TO COMMITTAL TO CARE

	Boys	Girls	Total	%	Cawson's Sample %
Committed at first appearance	30	5	35	45	31
Committed at second appearance	9	2	11	14	28
Committed at third appearance	7	2	9	11.5	18
Committed at fourth appearance	6	—	6	8	10
Committed at fifth appearance	7	2	9	11.5	12
Committed at sixth appearance	5	—	5	6	
Committed at seventh or more appearances	3	—	3	4	
	N	=	78*		

*Excludes one case for which we were unable to collect information.

v. LENGTH OF TIME THE CHILD HAS BEEN KNOWN TO THE SOCIAL SERVICE DEPARTMENT

	Boys	*Girls*	*Total*	*%*
/yr	20	3	23	24
1 — 1.11	13	1	14	18
2 — 2.11	8	2	10	13
3 — 3.11	2	2	4	5
4 — 4.11	3	—	3	4
5 — 5.11	5	1	6	8
6 — 6.11	5	1	6	8
7+	11	1	12	15
	67	11	78*	

*Excludes one case for which we were unable to collect information.

vi. PREVIOUS CARE EXPERIENCE

	Boys	*Girls*	*Total*	*%*
Remand in Care/Interim Care Order only	31	4	35	45
SI 1948 Children Act	13	3	16	21
Care Order	13	2	15	19
None	10	2	12	15
		N =	78*	

*Excludes one case for which we were unable to collect information.

Appendices

vii. FAMILY COMPOSITION

	Boys	*Girls*	*Total*	*%*
Natural parents	24	3	26	33
Mother alone	22	5	27	35
Father alone	4	2	6	8
Mother and stepfather	5	—	5	7
Father and stepmother	5	—	5	7
Mother and cohabitant	2	1	3	4
Father and cohabitant	1	—	1	1
Foster parents	1	—	1	1
No parental figures	3	—	3	4
	67	17	78*	

*Excludes one child for which we were unable to collect information.

viii. PLACEMENT IMMEDIATELY PRECEEDING CARE ORDER

	Boys	*Girls*	*Total*	*%*	*Cawson's Sample %*
Parents Home	21	—	21	27	53
Observation & Assessment Centre	29	5	34	43	28
Children's Home	10	1	11	14	
Community Home with Education	2	1	3	2	11
Hostel	3	1	4	5	
Remand Centre	1	2	3	4	3
Friends	1	1	2	3	5
	67	11	78*		

*Excludes one case for which we were unable to collect information.

ix. PLACEMENTS IMMEDIATELY AFTER CARE ORDER

	Boys	*Girls*	*Total*	*%*	*Cawson's Sample %*
Observation and Assessment Centre	32	5	37	48	38
Children's Home	10	1	11	14	7
Home Awaiting Placement	8	—	8	10	31
Home on Placement	7	1	8	10	
Community Home with Education	3	1	4	5	17
Hostel	2	1	3	4	2
Remand Centre	0	1	1	1	—
Other	5	1	6	8	5

N=78*

*Excludes one child on which we had no information.

x. PLACEMENTS AT THE END OF SIX MONTH FOLLOW UP

	Boys	*Girls*	*Total*	*%*	*Cawson's Sample %*
Observation and Assessment Centre	12	3	15	20	8
Community Home with Education	16	4	20	26	43
Children's Home	9	—	9	12	7
Other Residential School	3	—	3	4	6
Home as placement	10	1	11	14	
Home awaiting placement	4	—	4	5	24
Borstal Detention Centre	4	—	4	5	2
Hostel	5	1	6	8	3
Others	2	2	4	5	7
Absconded	1	—	1	1	

N=77*

*One child had the care order rescinded within the six month period and for one child we had no information.

78 children had a total of 161 placements during the six month period.

References

Adler, M. and Asquith, S. 1979. 'Discretion and Power' in discussion paper for S.S.R.C. Workshop on Discretionary Decision Making. Edinburgh, January, 1979.

Adler, M. and Asquith, S. (eds.) *Discretion and Welfare*. London: Heinemann, 1981

Becker, H. *Outsiders*. New York: Free Press, 1963.

Berlins, M. and Wansell, G. *Caught in the Act*. Harmondsworth: Penguin, 1974.

Bittner, E. 'The concept of organization' in Turner, R. (ed.), *Ethnomethodology*. Harmondsworth: Penguin, 1974.

Blaxter, M. *The Meaning of Disability*. London: Heinemann, 1976.

British Association of Social Workers. *The Social Work Task*. Birmingham: B.A.S.W., 1977.

Brody, S. *The Effectiveness of Sentencing*. Home Office Research Study No. 35. London: H.M.S.O., 1976.

Browne, E. 'Social Work Activities' in Stevenson, O. *et al* (eds.). *Social Service Teams: The Practitioner's View*. London: H.M.S.O., 1978.

Cawson, P. *Young Offenders in Care: Preliminary Report*. D.H.S.S. 1978. Unpublished.

Young offenders in Care: Part 2. D.H.S.S. 1979. Unpublished.

Central Council for Education and Training in Social Work. *Good Enough Parenting*. London: C.C.E.T.S.W., 1978.

Cicourel, A. *The Social Organization of Juvenile Justice*. London: Heinemann, 1976.

Cooper, J. 'Dilemmas in assessment and treatment' in Institute for the Study and Treatment of Delinquency (ed.), *Children Still in Trouble?* London: I.S.T.D., 1973.

Crosland, C. A. R. *The Future of Socialism*. London: Johnathan Cape, 1964.

Curnock, K. and Hardiker, P. *Towards Practice Theory*. London: Routledge and Kegan Paul, 1979.

Cypher, J. R. 'Social Reform and the Social Work Profession: What Hope for a Rapprochement?' in Jones, H. (ed.). *Towards a New*

Social Work. London: Routledge and Kegan Paul, 1975.

Department of Health and Social Security. *Children and Young Persons Act – Memorandum on a Survey by the Social Work Service*, D.H.S.S., 1972. Unpublished mimeo.

Children and Young Persons Act 1969 – Memorandum on a Further Survey by the Social Work Service. D.H.S.S., 1973. Unpublished mimeo

Emerson, R. *Judging Delinquents*. Chicago: Aldine, 1969.

Erikson, E. *Childhood and Society*. Harmondsworth: Penguin, 1965.

Etzioni, A. *Modern Organizations*. Englewood Cliffs: Prentice-Hall, 1964.

Field, E. *et al*. *Thirteen-year-old Approved School Boys in 1962*. Home Office Research Unit Report 11. London: H.M.S.O., 1971.

Filstead, W. J. (ed.) *Qualitative Methodology*. Chicago: Markham, 1970.

Garfinkel, H. '"Good" Organizational Reasons For "Bad" Clinic Records' in Turner, R. (ed.). *Ethnomethodology*. Harmondsworth: Penguin, 1974.

Giller, H. and Morris, A. 'Supervision Orders: The Routinization of Treatment'. *Howard Journal*, Vol. 17, No. 4 1978.

Grace, C. and Wilkinson, P. *Negotiating the Law*. London: Routledge and Kegan Paul, 1978.

Hall, S. *et al*. *Policing the Crisis*. London: Macmillan, 1978.

Hardiker, P. 'Social Work Ideologies in the Probation Service.' *British Journal of Social Work* (7) 2. vol. 7, No. 2, 1977.

Hardiker, P. and Webb D. 'Explaining Deviant Behaviour.' *Sociology* Vol. 13, No. 1, 1979.

Hazel, N. 'The Use of Family Placements in the Treatment of Delinquency.' Tutt, N. (ed.). *Alternative Strategies for Coping with Crime*. Oxford: Blackwell, 1978.

Hoghughi, M. *What's in a Name?: Some Consequences of the 1969 Children and Young Persons Act*. Aycliffe: 1973.

Troubled and Troublesome. London: Burnett Books in association with André Deutsch, 1978.

Home Office. *Children in Trouble*. Cmnd. 3601. London: H.M.S.O., 1968.

Home Office *et al*. *Children and Young Persons Act 1969: Observation on the Eleventh Report from the Expenditure Committee*. Cmnd. 6494. London: H.M.S.O., 1976.

House of Commons Expenditure Committee. *Eleventh Report, Children and Young Persons Act 1969*. Vol. 1 report, Vol. 2 evidence. H.C. 354: and ii. London: H.M.S.O., 1975.

Magistrates Association *et al*. *The Children and Young Persons Act 1969: Report of a Joint Working Party*. London: Association of County Councils, 1978.

122 *References*

Matza, D. *Delinquency and Drift*. New York: John Wiley and Sons, 1964.

May, D. 'Delinquency Control and the Treatment Model: Some Implications of Recent Legislation.' *British Journal of Criminology*, vol. 11, No. 4, 359–370, 197.

May, D. and Smith, G. *Gentlemen vs. Players. Lay-Professional Relations in the Administration of Juvenile Justice*. Paper presented at British Sociological Association, April, 1979.

May, J. S. *Youngsters in Court. Phase I*. Warwick: Warwickshire Social Services Department, 1977.

May, J.S. *Youngsters in Court. Phase II*. Warwick: Warwickshire Social Services Department, 1978.

Mayer, J. and Timms, N. *The Client Speaks*. London: Routledge and Kegan Paul, 1970.

Millham, S. *et al. After Grace – Teeth*. London: Human Context Books, 1975.

Morris, A. and Giller, H. *'Juvenile Justice and Social Work in Britain.'* Parker, H., (ed.). *Social Work and the Courts*. London: Edward Arnold, 1979.

Morris, C. 'The Children and Young Persons Act: Creating More Institutionalization.' *Howard Journal,* Vol. 16, No. 3, 154–158, 1978.

Packman, J. *Child Care: Needs and Numbers*. London: George Allen & Unwin, 1968.

Piliavin, M. and Briar, S. 'Police Encounters with Juveniles.' *American Journal of Sociology*, Vol. 70, No. 2, 206–214, 1964.

Pritchard, C. and Taylor, R. *Social Work: Reform or Revolution*. London: Routledge and Kegan Paul, 1978.

Rees, S. 'Defining Moral Worthiness: Grounds for Intervention in Social Work.' *Social Work Today* Vol. 7, No. 17, 203–6. *Social Work Face to Face*. London: Edward & Arnold, 1978.

Reid, W. and Epstein, L. *Task Centred Casework*, New York: Columbia University Press, 1972.

Sachs, H. 'Notes on Police Assessment of Moral Character.' *Studies in Social Interaction*. New York: Free Press, 1972.

Sainsbury, E. *Social Work with Families*. London: Routledge and Kegan Paul, 1975.

Schutz, A. *Collected papers I. The Problem of Social Reality*. The Hague: Martinus Nijhoff, 1962.

Smith, G. 'Discretionary Decision Making in Social Work', in

Adler, M. and Asquith, S. (eds.) *Discretion and Welfare*. London: Heinemann, 1981.

Smith, G. and Harris, R. 'Ideologies of Need and the Organization of Social Work Departments.' *British Journal of Social Work*. Vol. 2, No. 1.

Social Services Research and Intelligence Unit *First Year at Fairfield Lodge*. Portsmouth: S.S.R.I., 1976.

Stevenson, O. 'Metholodogy' *Social Service Teams: The Practitioner's View*. London: H.M.S.O., 1978.

Strauss, A. *et al. Psychiatric Ideologies and Institutions*. Glencoe: Free Press, 1964.

Sudnow, F. *Passing On: The Social Organization of Dying*. New York; Prentice-Hall, 1967.

Sugden, G. 'Care orders.' in *The Magistrate*, Vol. 28, No. 2, 1972.

Timms, N. *Casework in the Child Care Service*. London: Butterworths, 1969.

Tutt, N. *The Philosophy of Observation and Assessment*. Unpublished paper, D.H.S.S., 1977.

Walter, A. *Sent Away: A Study of Young Offenders in Care*. Saxon House: Farnborough, 1978.

Weber, M. *The Theory of Social and Economic Organizations*. New York: Free Press, 1947.

West, D. J. and Farrington, D. *Who Becomes Delinquent?* London: Heinemann, 1973.

Zander, M. 'What Happens to Young Offenders in Care.' *New Society*, 24 July, 1975.

Zimmermann, D. 'The Practicalities of Rule Use.' Douglas J. D. (ed.). *Understanding Everyday Life*. London: Routledge & Kegan Paul, 1971.

'Fact as a Practical Accomplishment.' Turner, R. (ed.). *Ethnomethodology*. Harmondsworth: Penguin, 1974.

Index